Tracking Down the Holy Ghost

Reflections on Love and Longing

Frank T. Griswold

Church Publishing

NEW YORK

Church Publishing
19 East 34th Street
New York, NY 10016
www.churchpublishing.org

Cover design by Jennifer Kopec, 2Pug Design
Typeset by Denise Hoff

Library of Congress Cataloging-in-Publication Data

Names: Griswold, Frank T., 1937– author.
Title: Tracking down the Holy Ghost : reflections on love and
    longing / Frank T. Griswold.
Description: New York : Church Publishing, 2017.
Identifiers: LCCN 2017033517 (print) | LCCN 2017038597 (ebook)
    | ISBN 9780819233660 (ebook) | ISBN 9780819233653 (pbk.)
Subjects: LCSH: Spirituality--Christianity. | Spiritual life--
    Christianity. | Spiritual formation.
Classification: LCC BV4501.3 (ebook) | LCC BV4501.3 .G746
    2017 (print) | DDC 248.4/83--dc23
LC record available at https://lccn.loc.gov/2017033517

Printed in Canada

Contents

To the Reader

Flannery O'Connor once described the serious writer's task as one of following lines of spiritual motion from the surface of life into that deep place where revelation occurs: "This is simply an attempt to track down the Holy Ghost through a tangle of human suffering and aspiration and idiocy. It is an attempt that should be pursued with gusto." It seems to me this task belongs not only to the serious writer; tracking down the Holy Ghost is an ongoing work that belongs to us all.

As long as I can remember I have been following those elusive lines of spiritual motion. They have led me through my own tangle into places I would never have imagined myself going: from the day of my baptism, through the various chapters of my life as a student, a parish priest, a husband and father, the Bishop of Chicago, until I found myself as Presiding Bishop of the Episcopal Church, and now moving on through a time of continuing discovery.

Though I spend my days as a teacher and preacher, and am thus presumably conversant with theology and the soul wisdom of many who have gone before, at heart I remain a seeker: a person under construction, tracking down the Holy Ghost, and with gusto! It has become ever clearer to me that all things have the potential to reveal the Divine and the mystery of love that lies at the heart of the universe, a mystery that has been variously named and understood across the centuries. For me, this mystery bears the name God.

"You have made us for yourself, O Lord, and our heart is restless until it rests in you," declared Saint Augustine of Hippo many centuries ago. These words capture something of the longing that has been planted deep within us—a longing and a restlessness that, in my experience, finds its truest satisfaction when we are open to the sense that there is something more that draws us beyond ourselves.

Over the years I have sought to be, in the words of Anglican priest and poet George Herbert, a "tracker of God's ways": that is to follow the lines of motion through the seasons of my life, and to record some of what I have learned along the way. These pages are the fruit of my effort to gather up the fragments from what I have learned about myself, about love and longing, about God and God's ways with us. If you are drawn, as I have been, to follow lines of spiritual motion, perhaps the stories and reflections in these pages will be an encouragement. You may discover revelatory moments in your own life you have overlooked because they seem so ordinary and mundane, or ill-suited to our notions of God and how God ought to behave.

In earlier times books were intended to be read aloud. Each word was not only taken in by the eye but also deliberately pronounced. While speed-reading has its uses, it is not meant to replace the meditative practice that was once the norm. Baron Friedrich von Hügel, a wise spiritual guide to many of the last century, including the English mystic Evelyn Underhill, used the image of a cow quietly and unhurriedly munching her way through a field to describe this practice of reading as meditation. I am sure it is not by accident that the ancients often used the verb *ruminare*, to ruminate, to describe such reflective reading. This book might be approached in that "chewing over" fashion. It is divided into stories and reflections of various lengths to suggest that you might stop and linger as suits you, allowing you to take in the words more deeply in relation to your own understanding and experience.

I offer these pages to fellow seekers in humble and grateful recognition of the many pilgrims who have sustained and strengthened me along the way through their faithfulness, friendship, and wise counsel. Without their continuing encouragement, and sometimes correction, I might well wander off the path.

Frank T. Griswold

Listening to Your Life

Listen to your life. See it for the fathomless mystery it is. In the boredom and pain of it, no less than in the excitement and gladness: touch, taste, smell your way to the holy and hidden heart of it, because in the last analysis all moments are key moments, and life itself is grace.

—Frederick Buechner

A young couple I will call Davis and Linda were members of a congregation I once served. They met after college while serving in the Peace Corps in Guatemala. Love bloomed, and they married upon their return to the United States. As both had been raised in Episcopal households, when they had their first child—perhaps pressured somewhat by both sets of grandparents—they came to see me to discuss the baptism of their newborn son. Adam was duly baptized, and after that Davis and Linda became a regular part of our church community.

When Davis made an appointment with me, telling me he had something he needed to talk about, I hoped it was not something like an upsetting medical diagnosis. He arrived at the appointed hour and moved quickly to the point. "It's about God," he said. "God seems so distant . . . like an abstraction. I *say* I believe in God, but where is he?"

Davis, who was a teacher at a nearby Quaker school, told me he was regularly exposed to the worship that was part of school life. There he experienced the periods of reverential silence. He said that during those times he felt that some force beyond himself was tugging at him. Then, when he came to church on Sunday, the formal language of the liturgy felt stilted and foreign to him: *Our Father . . . Creator of Heaven and Earth . . . Hallowed be thy name . . .*

Davis was struggling and restless in his spirit. He was describing a state common to many. They—we—have a sense something very significant is going on, perhaps under the surface of things—something they might name as life force, energy, mystery, or even coincidence. He longed to connect with some external force he named as *God,* but it eluded him. We sat quietly together. After a time I suggested that his very questioning was a sign that God, who seemed so remote, was the One provoking him to seek God. I told him we somehow get the idea that a relationship with God means we have to strain toward something cosmic and other. Not so. God is close at hand, clothed in the events that constitute our personal history. Frequently the Divine is lurking unseen under the cover of things that seem utterly mundane.

"We seek you, O God, because you have already found us," observed Saint Augustine. And where does God find us? God finds us in the ebb and flow of our own lives. I told Davis that God is closer to us than we are to our own selves, and perhaps God was inviting him through his very questioning to look for God not in the elevated language of the liturgy but in the immediacy of his own daily life.

Saint Augustine also asked, "How can you draw close to God if you are far from your own self?" For Augustine, self-awareness and knowledge of God are one unified experience. Thus, when we are out of touch with ourselves, it is very difficult to get in touch with God. And, how do we know ourselves? One way is to pay close attention to what is going on within and around us, as I advised Davis to do. We know ourselves by *reading the scripture of our own lives.*

Just as the Bible is a collection of stories recounting human encounters with the Divine, our lives too are a series of stories in which the ordinary has the potential to reveal the extraordinary: intimations of the presence of God. What seasons have we passed through? What joys and sorrows have overtaken us? What accomplishments and failures have we experienced? God has been present in all of this, though possibly hidden and unacknowledged.

Surely, this commandment that I am commanding you today is not too hard for you, nor is it too far away. It is not in heaven, that you should say, "Who will go up to heaven for us, and get it for us so that we may hear it and observe it?" Neither is it beyond the sea, that you should say, "Who will come to the other side of the sea for us, and get it for us so that we may hear it and observe it?" No, the word is very near to you; it is in your mouth and in your heart for you to observe. —Deuteronomy 30:11–14

Hearing the intimate word that is already present within us, waiting to be born into consciousness, involves being intensely present to our own lives, intensely present to the events that are daily making us uniquely who we are. Hearing this intimate word means accepting that the hidden treasure of God's intent can be found in the soil of our own existence, in the field of our own heart. If we are not present to our own lives, then we cannot be present to this word.

Sometimes we cannot hear the word because of our own anxieties, our own self-distancing, our own unwillingness to welcome the word as it is present within us. Yet, if we are faithful, the Spirit turns over the soil more and more deeply, and the word finally can emerge into consciousness and be lived in a whole-hearted way.

The word of God planted in all of us is one of creativity and boundless vitality, and appears throughout scripture and in the life of the early Christian community. As recorded in the Book of Acts, it grew and prevailed, confounding a group of ill-prepared disciples who were trying to catch up with it, presenting them with new situations that required their response. The word constantly pulled them forward, expanding their notions of what it meant to be persons of faith, enlarging their previous notions of God's ways, obliging them to embrace something new.

In the Abrahamic tradition, speech is a medium of divine self-disclosure. Therefore, the fundamental stance of the person of faith is to listen. In scripture we read: *Hear O Israel . . . Speak, Lord, for your servant is listening . . . Be it unto me according to your word . . . Hear what the Spirit is saying to the churches.*

The Hebrew word *dabar* means not only word or speech but also event and circumstance. Divine speech, therefore, is not only spoken: it happens. We experience and live the word, in ways both trivial and remarkable.

And the Word became flesh and lived among us . . .

Perhaps the Incarnation—the Word taking flesh in the person of Jesus—is the most dramatic instance of word becoming an historical event. The Divine Word, who spoke creation into being, took flesh in the person of Jesus, and inhabits, as Spirit, the whole of creation, including all of humanity.

A sentence I sometimes say to myself in an effort to remain open and available to God's ever-active word comes from James Finley, who was a disciple of Thomas Merton. *"A simple openness to the next human moment brings us into union with God in Christ."*

———————

"Obsculta, o fili . . . Listen carefully, my son, to the master's instructions, and attend to them with the ear of your heart." These are the opening words of the prologue to his *Rule for Monks*, written by St. Benedict in the sixth century. The Rule has formed and guided the response of countless men and women to the call of Christ. Taken as a whole, it is about ordered and careful listening: listening with the ear of the heart, the heart being understood not simply as the seat of our emotions but as the core and center of our personhood. What we are listening for is God's word, which comes to us in various forms. Sometimes it is a clear and direct personal address, and sometimes it comes in puzzling disguise. Then again, it can come as a question to be lived without the security of an answer or easy resolution.

In the prologue, St. Benedict goes on to describe the monastery as "a school of the Lord's service" in which the heart, which at first may be bound by fear, is expanded through careful listening and overflows "with the inexpressible delight of love." The process of expansion or, more properly, transformation, is accomplished by careful listening: listening to the Abbot who represents the living Word who is Christ; listening to the members of the community with particular emphasis on the elders and the youngest who, in different ways, are bearers of the Word; listening to visitors with their insights and words of criticism as coming from the Lord; listening to the living word of scripture in the context of common prayer woven into the rhythms of the day, the week, the seasons, the feasts and fasts which make up the liturgical year; listening to the word revealed through the labor of one's hands and the practice of *lectio*, that is meditative reading. In all these ways a listening heart is formed, and conformed over time to the pattern of Christ.

During my years as a student at St. Paul's School, a boarding school in Concord, New Hampshire, I read a biography of St. Benedict and found myself drawn to him and to his Rule. The Rule gave me a vision of an ordered life, rooted and grounded in patterns of prayer. I was experiencing chaos in my own family life; I understand now that in the Rule I had found a stabilizing and grounding counterbalance. St. Benedict has remained a special companion and friend ever since.

Over the years, I have maintained close ties with monastic communities in both Episcopal and Roman Catholic churches. In fact, members of religious orders have been my most significant guides and wisdom figures. It strikes me as paradoxical that those who have vowed themselves to what can appear to be an extreme and life-denying pattern of existence can become men and women endowed with a remarkable breadth of compassion and the ability to allow for the vagaries of our humanity. Through the depth of their prayer and their struggles with their own unruly natures, they often develop an acute sense of the crooked ways in which God's grace overtakes and illumines us. Though the monastic life is shaped by rules, it often produces in those who live it deeply a quality of freedom that allows them to look beyond the rules and discover that God's grace can manifest itself in wild and unexpected ways. The Trappist monk

Thomas Merton is a case in point. While living in one of the most outwardly severe monastic environments, he learned to embrace the world with a cosmic heart and to find intimations of God's grace in places that sometimes strained Christian orthodoxy.

⌒

Unsurprisingly, when we read the scripture of our own lives we tend to be highly selective in what we care to remember and bring to consciousness. We easily live with the fantasy that if the Divine is anywhere, it is only in those things we consider positive and filled with virtue. Quite frankly, there are many things I would prefer never to recall: failures, embarrassments, diminishments, things I have done I ought not to have done and can now never undo. However, I have learned that my growth, my more acute shaping, is often born out of struggle and suffering. Reading the scripture of my life involves asking God to reveal to me how life's darker moments and painful memories can at times be transmuted and lead to deeper insight and blessing. The monks and members of religious orders I have known along the way have been incredibly important in teaching me to find and embrace traces of the Divine in unlikely circumstances.

My first experience with a monastic guide occurred at age fifteen when I was at St. Paul's. One of the clergy on the faculty noticed in me a burgeoning spiritual awareness and decided I would benefit from "spiritual direction." I had no idea what he was talking about, but as it would give me special permission to leave school and take the train to Boston for an afternoon, I responded to his urging with alacrity. He sent me off to see the Cowley Fathers, as the Society of Saint John the Evangelist, a monastic community within the Episcopal Church, was informally known. I learned some years later that the Superior of the Society had been appalled that a fifteen-year-old needed spiritual direction and, mercifully, had assigned me to the Rev. Alfred L. Pedersen, SSJE, surely one of the most worldly and sophisticated members of the community. Father Pedersen knew just how to deal with an overwrought adolescent whose newly discovered religious fervor found its outlet in the devotional practices associated with Anglo-Catholicism. He, so to speak, calmed me down. I said, "Father, I prepare for my confessions for at least an hour." He replied, "Given your tendency toward scrupulosity, I think ten minutes of preparation is quite sufficient." He was patient with me, tempered my rigorous spirit with his gentle good humor, and in many ways became a spiritual father to me.

Another important guide along the way was Father Damasus Winsen, the prior of Mount Saviour, a Roman Catholic Benedictine monastery near Elmira, New York. He was a wise and seasoned monk originally from the Abbey of Maria Laach in Germany. I first met Father Damasus soon after my ordination when I was invited to make a retreat with a group of newly ordained Roman Catholic priests. One afternoon Father Damasus invited me for a walk. Of course, I was flattered that I had caught his attention. As we started off through one of the pastures surrounding the monastery I decided to dazzle him with my grasp of the intricacies of monastic liturgy. I asked a complicated question about the responsories in the monastic breviary. My question was intended to reveal that, though I was an Anglican, I knew more about his liturgical tradition than most Roman Catholics. He saw right through me and my efforts to validate myself in his eyes. He stopped in his tracks, turned toward me, placed his hands on my shoulders, smiled, and said gently: "Oh Franziskus, you are so very, very Anglican." In that moment I felt his compassion in the face of my tortured efforts to justify myself as an Anglican in his Roman Catholic world. I felt exposed, deeply known, and embraced just as I was.

In the years that followed, I continued to go on retreat to Mount Saviour and the friendship between the prior and the self-conscious Anglican deepened. He always addressed me using his mother tongue, as "Franziskus," the German form of Francis. In the evening after Compline he often would say to me: "Franziskus, come to *Casa Abbatiale* but first get a corkscrew from the kitchen." "*Casa Abbatiale*" was a euphemism for a renovated chicken coop that had become his residence, "the Abbot's House," when his cell in the monastery became too filled with books and papers for comfortable habitation. As he poured each of us a glass of his Riesling, I poured out my soul and stood ready to receive his wise counsel.

Father Damasus's successor as prior, Father Martin Boler, also played a significant role in my life. Father Martin was a medical doctor by training and knew a great deal about both body and soul. Once, as I concluded making a particularly searching and labored confession, rich in self-accusation, he smiled at me and said gently: "Frank, welcome to the human condition." His words, and the way he said them, conveyed divine compassion well beyond the formal words of absolution, which he then pronounced. I later came to understand that I had spent the week of retreat time scrutinizing the history of my sinfulness in a spirit of self-directed judgment rather than by having been led by the Holy Spirit to see my failings in the light of God's merciful love. Father Martin's words made me realize that for my retreats in the future I would need a guide and companion along the way.

The next year, a fellow priest told me of his experience making an eight-day retreat at the nearby Jesuit spiritual center in Wernersville, Pennsylvania. The retreat was structured around a daily consultation with a spiritual director who would listen alongside you to the stirrings of the Spirit and focus your prayer, largely with passages of scripture, for the next day. The structure appealed to me immediately, as I saw that the director would stand as a guard against self-deception or going off in wrong directions.

I signed up for the retreat with some trepidation as I had been led to believe that Jesuit spirituality was harsh and rigorous. In my mind's eye, Jesuits all wore rimless glasses and were possessed of an intensity that admitted no levity. I was in for a real surprise. Peter Foley, the priest assigned to guide me, was a man of my own age with a smiling face, horn-rimmed glasses, and a mustache that looked much like the one I sported in those days.

The eight days were an overwhelming experience during which I was confronted by a sense of my own inner poverty and God's overwhelming generosity and love. The words of Mary's song, recorded in the Gospel of Luke, became the heart of my prayer. "My soul proclaims the greatness of the Lord, my spirit rejoices in God my savior; for he has looked with favor on his lowly servant." Paradoxically, an awareness of my own "lowliness" became the gateway to gratitude and joy. And so, with a sense of deep blessing the retreat ended, or so I thought.

I went to bed that final night feeling peaceful, and eager to return home in the morning. Then, well before dawn, I awoke and found myself in turmoil, feeling isolated and fearful. Why was this happening to me? Why was the joy and blessing of what I had experienced during my retreat being undermined? I had seen Peter for the last time the previous evening and now was on my own. I prayed fervently that God would explain what was happening. I thought if only I could figure it out and make sense of it I would feel better. I felt anxious that the gifts and blessings of the week would now be lost. I asked God—*why?*—and pleaded for rescue. Finally, exhausted, I gave up my struggle.

At that moment, deep within me I heard a voice: *I am with you in the midst of your suffering. If you try to distance yourself from your suffering you will distance yourself from me. You can only find me in the midst of what you are experiencing.*

With these words, I suddenly knew that Christ was with me in the midst of my turmoil. I had been joined in my struggle, but not rescued. Christ consoled me, not with an explanation for my feelings, but with an infusion of his own confidence and courage. Curiously, I felt that the grace and gift of the retreat had been not only confirmed, but deepened.

So often when we are wounded by suffering or loss we desperately search for an explanation: "Why is this happening to me?" We presume that knowing a reason for it will lessen the pain we are enduring. I find explanations provide little comfort for someone who is suffering. The gift is the companionship of One who himself knew suffering and is therefore able to join us as an intimate friend and companion in the midst of our pain and confusion. Brother Roger of Taizé observed that a wound is the place where Christ is most deeply present.

"The Lord bade me keep my mind in hell and not despair," declared St. Silouan, a monk of Mt. Athos, in a time of great trial. These words, which urge us to remain steadfast in the midst of what may seem like Hell, sound extreme, but they have been a rock to stand on that I have shared with others in their times of suffering and severe testing.

This first eight-day retreat led me in the next year to make the full thirty-day retreat according to the Spiritual Exercises of St. Ignatius Loyola, and then to be trained in giving the Exercises to others. I had been befriended by Ignatius as I had been by Benedict, and he led me forward as another companion and friend.

During this time I met Father Gary Brophy, who was also on the staff at Wernersville. Gary soon became another wise guide and friend in the Spirit. He could be both tough and tender. His direct and urgent manner owed in part to the fact that his health was compromised by kidney disease, which required regular dialysis. When he was transferred to the Jesuit community at Creighton University in Omaha I began to go there for my annual retreats, as I do to this day. Gary died several years after moving to Creighton, and I was invited to speak at the vigil the night before his funeral. I described him as "the keeper of the secrets of my heart." This description resonated with many of his brother Jesuits.

I continue to be grateful for these wise guides. They are with me still, beyond this life in the communion of saints.

———

*The gift of baptism is the Holy Spirit. But the Holy Spirit
is Christ himself dwelling in the hearts of the faithful.*
—Dietrich Bonhoeffer

Carl Jung once observed that "the western attitude with its emphasis on the object tends to fix the ideal—Christ—in its outward aspect and thus robs it of its mysterious relation to the inner man. . . . Too few people have experienced the divine image as the innermost possession of their souls. Christ only meets them from without—never from within the soul."

I hear these words as an invitation to enter into a deep interior relationship with Christ, which is to know Christ as the truth that indwells us, the truth not as information or a proposition we can store somewhere, but as something to be lived in an ever-unfolding relationship. This lifelong process depends upon our willingness to pay attention to the ebb and flow of our lives. It is within the circumstances of our lives that the Spirit of Christ meets us.

Our relationship with Christ, as well as being for our own growth and delight, also has social consequences as we are drawn forward beyond our personal experience of God and called to embrace others. The Spirit of Christ at work in us is the agent of God's love, and love, by its very nature, must give itself away.

———

When confronted by something I would rather avoid than face, I recall the words of the French Jesuit, Pierre Teilhard de Chardin: "By means of all created things, without exception, the Divine assails us, penetrates us and molds us." God may be shaping and molding me even in trying and unwelcome circumstances, and I am forcibly liberated from my efforts at self-construction. As a paleontologist as well as a priest, Teilhard de Chardin saw creation as an ever-unfolding revelation of the Divine, and as a witness to the presence of the cosmic Christ in whom all matter converges and attains its true end. For him all creation revealed the Divine.

Remembering

We are made, they say,
by what we remember
    and choose to forget.

Our memories are our treasure,
as well, Pandora's Box.
Within them lies the mystery
    of who we are,
    and how we came to be.

We release them like ghosts
from long-sealed tombs.
The stone rolls back and out comes
    Lazarus smelling like death
    or the shade of our mother.

Wanting more
we excavate our plot of time passed
like archaeologists
fingering carefully through the rubble.
    Old bowls, broken as promises.
    Cloth, woven to last.

Or we wait.
Sometimes we simply wait
as for snowdrops
    that withstood cold and the hard frost of winter
    and now, improbably, emerge.

We find our memories
or they find us
and attach themselves
    like extra appendages.

Better to search, I say
to find what wants to be found
and, of course, what prefers
    to remain
    hidden.   —Barbara Leix Braver

Dr. Karl Menninger, one of the great pioneers in the field of mental health, once observed that from his perspective a primary cause of mental illness lies in our inability to forgive ourselves for not being perfect. Paul tells us that God's love is poured into our hearts by the Holy Spirit. How sad it is when our preoccupation with our imperfections undermines our ability to make room for God's love.

George Herbert was an Anglican country parson who lived near Salisbury, England, in the seventeenth century. Herbert struggled with the tenaciousness of God's love and our unwillingness to welcome it because of our preoccupation with our inadequacies and imperfections.

In Herbert's poem "Love III," we hear Christ's voice. The poem wonderfully captures Herbert's resistance to the unyielding force of Love, who rejects the poet's desperate invocations of his lack of worth. Backed into a corner, the poet's final effort before surrender is his offer to engage in some act of service to justify himself in his own eyes as worthy of Love's attention. Love overrules this final ploy on the poet's part and cuts him off, declaring "you must sit down, and taste my meat":

> Love bade me welcome, yet my soul drew back,
>   Guilty of dust and sin.
> But quick-ey'd Love, observing me grow slack
>   From my first entrance in,
> Drew nearer to me, sweetly questioning
>   If I lack'd anything.
> "A guest," I answer'd, "worthy to be here";
>   Love said, "You shall be he."
> "I, the unkind, the ungrateful? ah my dear,
>   I cannot look on thee."
> Love took my hand and smiling did reply,
>   "Who made the eyes but I?"
> "Truth, Lord, but I have marr'd them; let my shame
>   Go where it doth deserve."
> "And know you not," says Love, "who bore the
>   blame?"
> "My dear, then I will serve."
> "You must sit down," says Love, "and taste my meat."
>   So I did sit and eat.

In the middle of the last century, Sergius Bolshakoff, a prominent Russian Orthodox theologian, made his way deep into the forests of Finland to a remote monastery that had been established by a community of elderly Russian monks in exile. In his account of the visit he describes his conversations with Father John who, because of his great age and many years of monastic life, was looked upon with particular respect. Before taking his leave, Bolshakoff asked Father John one final question: "How can we find our way in life, Father?" Father John replied: "The very circumstances of our lives will show us the way." Father John's years of monastic observance had taught him that the vagaries of life as we experience them are the medium of Divine encounter and revelation.

The very circumstances of our lives will show us the way. These words have become something of a touchstone for me, and a reminder of the importance of attending to the present moment. I know from experience that God addresses us personally all the time, and not just around the edges. As we recognize God's presence in the events of our lives, we are reading the lived scripture of our own experience. The Spirit blows where it chooses, Jesus tells us in the Gospel of John, and therefore God's activity is in no way confined to the realm of the sacred. As we accustom ourselves to listen for God's voice in the midst of the complexities and challenges of the daily, we may find that we are no longer alone. Rather, we are companioned along the way by the One who is more intimate to us than we are to our own selves.

Are You a Michelob Man?

Shortly after I became a bishop I went off for my annual retreat—an extended period of time for prayer and reflection. I headed to Omaha, Nebraska, because Gary Brophy had recently been transferred there. It was important to me that someone I already knew, and who had known me in the past, be my guide and companion as I sought to find my grounding in this new, overwhelming chapter of my life. Anxious that my time in Omaha be fruitful, I took with me several books of prayers and other resources. Each day I read and prayed. The harder I prayed and the more I read, the more God seemed distant and absent. Day after day nothing seemed to be happening, and I grew more and more frustrated. At this turning point in my ministry I felt terribly in need of a deep sense of God's presence and support. The only voice I heard was that of silence.

One afternoon I walked by a soup kitchen attached to a center for homeless people not far from where I was staying. As I stood in front of the door I remembered some advice of St. Ignatius of Loyola, in his "Rules for Discernment," included in his *Spiritual Exercises:* "When you find yourself in a place of desolation, act against the desolation that has overtaken you." In other words, if you are feeling isolated and depressed, don't shut yourself off from others. Don't allow yourself to become a prisoner of your negative emotions. Instead, do something quite contrary to the way you feel. Make yourself reach out to someone else. Reaching out may require great effort because desolation and self-pity can provide their own dark comfort.

With this in mind, I decided to enter the center and offer to help serve meals. I approached the person who seemed to be in charge and told him I wanted to help. He looked at me and said, "Son, you can help us by sitting down with our other guests and having a big plate of pancakes." In that moment I realized he had taken a measure of me in my old sweatshirt and jeans and thought I was one of the center's guests. This did nothing to ease my feelings of desolation. I went back to my room, feeling God's absence more acutely than ever. I tried to do more reading. I went and sat in front of the tabernacle in the chapel and prayed with some anxiety, knowing there were only two days left before my retreat ended.

The next morning I went to see Gary and told him what had happened the day before. His advice was very simple. "Go back to the center and tell them who you are." So, that afternoon I returned and told the new person in charge that I wanted to volunteer. He said: "You can wash dishes, but if you want to do more you are going to have to talk to Sister Pat."

A few minutes later a feisty-looking woman approached me

at the sink and handed me an enormous soup kettle in need of scrubbing. "Who on earth are you?" she asked. Remembering what Gary had advised, I knew this was my moment. I said: "I am Frank Griswold, the Bishop of Chicago." Sister Pat was not impressed. She simply said, "When you have finished we can have a cup of coffee." I scrubbed away and when I was finished Sister Pat reappeared with coffee mugs. We stepped out into the sunny courtyard and she told me about the work of the center and soup kitchen. As we talked I became aware of one of the guests—a man probably in his late thirties—standing near us. He was wearing glasses, but the right lens was missing. There was an eagerness about him, and I sensed that he wanted to enter into our conversation. Suddenly he broke in.

"Are you a Michelob Man?" Surprised by his question, I awkwardly replied, "No, I usually drink wine."

He said: "You are the man from Chicago with the gift for words." I was startled. This seemed very mysterious to me but I said nothing.

"This is Patrick Henderson, one of our regular guests," said Sister Pat.

As Patrick walked away from us, I asked Sister Pat if she had noticed that his glasses were missing a lens.

"Yes," she said. "At some point I hope we can attend to that." I told her that I would like to pay for it. "That would be great," she responded.

That night the encounter with Patrick Henderson stayed with me. I woke up very early the next morning, eager to return to the center to help serve breakfast. Something about our encounter the previous day made me hope I would see Patrick.

Back at the center I was again assigned to washing dishes. Patrick was nowhere in sight. As I washed the last mug the door opened and Patrick appeared. He saw me and with a broad smile on his face, called out: "Frank!" He knew my name, much to my surprise, and my heart filled with joy. He sat down for breakfast and when he finished his coffee and pancakes I followed him out onto the street. I told him I was returning to Chicago the next morning and that meeting him had been important to me.

I remember speaking those words with great feeling and being surprised by the strength of my own emotions.

Patrick stopped and looked at me. Then he said: "Thank you, Frank. Thank you for all you have done." I found myself overwhelmed by his words and turned away with tears in my eyes.

As Patrick walked away from me I wondered why I had been so deeply moved by our encounter. What was going on in me to provoke such a strong response? Then I remembered the parable in the Gospel of Matthew where Jesus tells us that when we serve the most vulnerable and needy we are serving him. "Truly I tell you, just as you did it to one of the least of these . . . you did it to me." I suddenly realized that I had met not simply a homeless man but Jesus. In my desperate search for Jesus in all the books I had brought with me, and in my efforts to stir up my own emotions in prayer, Christ had decided to reveal himself to me in Patrick. Perhaps when I offered the simple gift of having Patrick's eyeglasses repaired this had been an act of service not only to him but to Jesus himself. This event taught me a great deal about God's ability to draw near to us through things that happen to us and people we meet along the way: the daily and the ordinary. It struck me then that in some way my ability to recognize Jesus in Patrick Henderson was the consequence of my seemingly fruitless prayer. God had answered me, though not as I had expected.

Several years after this experience, I preached at a church in Rockford, Illinois, on the Feast of St. Michael and All Angels. I described angels as ministers of God's presence and unexpected messengers, and told them the story of my encounter with Patrick Henderson. After the service a woman in the congregation introduced herself to me. She told me she worked at the homeless shelter sponsored by the parish and that the center had a guest named Patrick Henderson. I asked her to inquire of him if he remembered meeting "the man from Chicago with the gift of words." She called back several days later and, indeed, it was the same Patrick Henderson.

I was eager to see Patrick again and made a plan to take him out to lunch. Some weeks later I met him at the center and asked if there was any particular place he wanted to go. Outback Steakhouse was his choice, and so off we went. We spoke a bit about how his life had gone since our last meeting. I asked him why he had left Omaha for Rockford, and he told me it felt safer to him.

After lunch I told him I wanted to give him a present as a token of our friendship and asked if there was something he would particularly like to have. He thought for a moment and then responded, "A pocket watch." We scoured the local stores without success. Patrick sensed my disappointment and said, "Frank, the watch really doesn't matter. The real gift is that you wanted to give me one." I left him back at the shelter. That was the last time I saw him. Looking back on the afternoon I have a sense that I had entertained an angel. As the Letter to the Hebrews has it: "Do not neglect to show hospitality to strangers, for by doing that some have entertained angels without knowing it." (Hebrews 13:2)

Many Patrick Hendersons have appeared in my life, but some I didn't recognize because I was not paying attention and available to their presence.

Across the years I have learned that prayer is an interior orientation of openness and receptivity to God's mystery as it impinges upon our lives. We are drawn out of ourselves into an expanded consciousness that allows us to meet what life sets before us such that we can both receive and respond. I agree with the English mystic Evelyn Underhill that there is no such thing as coincidence; rather, we are seeing God's universe caught in the act of rhyming.

Indeed, the very circumstances of our lives do show us the way.

Some years after my encounter with Patrick, the director of a diocesan-supported shelter for homeless men in Chicago invited me to speak to his guests about my life as a bishop. I thought this an unlikely topic for this particular audience but wanted to lend my support to the work of the shelter. On the appointed evening, after a particularly draining day,

I drove to a depressed area of the city and found my way to the church hall where the meeting was to take place. A dozen or so men sat on folding chairs in a circle and I joined them, filled with misgivings. I started describing to them some of my responsibilities. To my surprise, they seemed quite interested so I went on in some detail about the ins and outs of my days. When I finished one of the men said: "He has a heavy burden to carry. Let's pray for him." They all leapt up and surrounded and hugged me. As they stood in a circle one man prayed fervently that God would keep me safe and support me in my work, and they all replied with a resounding *AMEN!*

Their care and concern for me, when their lives were so unsettled and their futures so unsure, overwhelmed me. Once again, Christ had caught me by surprise and chosen to show up where I did not expect to meet him. What had begun as the fulfillment of an obligation had been transformed into an experience of grace and blessing.

Many questions in our lives do not yield immediate answers. This lesson has not been easy for me to learn. Sometimes resolution is long in coming and we have to go through extended periods of uncertainty and endure the painful burden of not knowing. Sometimes the presenting question is simply a prelude to a further question and prepares the way for a more profound and consequential resolution. Rainer Maria Rilke's words of counsel to a young poet, which have been helpful to many over the years since he wrote them, have been an encouragement to me to live life's questions with patience rather than force answers out of my anxious need for resolution.

Letters to a Young Poe

. . . be patient toward all that is unsolved in your heart
and try to love the questions themselves
like locked rooms
and like books that are written in a very foreign tongue.
Do not now seek the answers,
which cannot be given you,
because you would not be able to live them.
And the point is, to live everything.
Live the questions now.
Perhaps then,
you will gradually, without noticing it,
live along some distant day into the answer.

—Rainer Maria Rilke

Gathering the Fragments

*Who am I, O Lord God, and what is my house, that you
have brought me thus far? And yet this was a small thing
in your eyes . . .*   —2 Samuel 7:18

This prayer of King David has become very much my own.
As I stand at this point in my life, I look back with gratitude
and wonder over all that has passed, and yet I know that the
journey continues. *This is still not far enough.* I take with me
into the future—which has yet to be revealed—all that I have
experienced and learned from my life thus far.

I am often asked if I am "enjoying retirement." To this
I respond that I am not retired. Rather, I am *pensioned.* I
learned this distinction in a conversation with a professor
at the Seminario Teológico Evangélico in Matanzas, Cuba.
I was spending a term teaching at this interdenominational
seminary and when I told him I was retired he protested: *¡No!
¡Pensionado!*

I continue to be active and responsive to what life puts
before me, and I am eager for new opportunities for discovery,
growth, and service. However, unlike the patriarchs of the Old
Testament, I do not expect to live into my second century. At this
juncture, I have a sense that it is important to stand back and
reflect upon my life, to gather up the fragments of its various
seasons and distill from them whatever insight and wisdom they
may contain. Where to begin? It makes sense for my distillation
to begin with a retracing of some of the paths my life has taken.
Of course, I no longer consciously remember the first notable
events of my life, and I rely upon what I have been told.

My mortal body drew its first breath on September 18, 1937, and then, on January 1, 1938, as a prelude to a New Year's Day party, I was baptized in the home of my paternal grandmother. The day was chosen not because it was, according to the calendar of the Book of Common Prayer, The Feast of the Circumcision of Christ or, as the day is now more delicately titled, The Holy Name of Our Lord Jesus Christ, but because it was the hundredth anniversary of my great-grandfather's birth. As a token of my incorporation into the risen body of Christ I was presented not with a Bible or Prayer Book, as one might expect. Instead, my gift was a cigarette box engraved with my name and that of my great-grandfather and the significant dates so that I would keep ever in mind why I was baptized on that particular day.

This was during the largely unmourned era of what we might call "cultural religion." My family was by tradition Episcopalian and a nearby rector had been summoned to do the deed. As seen from the outside, this was a fully controlled event, orchestrated by my grandmother. However, unbeknownst to her, and certainly to me as an infant, at its heart it was a celebration of God's love. Before it is a ritual of incorporation or promise of discipleship, baptism is an act of love: God loving us "madly"—as the Eastern Orthodox religious tradition would say—simply because we are. In baptism God declares, through sign and symbol and the community of faith gathered around the font or standing at the water's edge, or in my case, beside the large bowl on my grandmother's table: *You are my daughter, my son, my beloved. In you I take pleasure and delight.*

As water was poured over my head while I lay cradled in the priest's arms, I had no idea what was going on, and in no way could my baptism have been construed as an expression of my faith. The baptism of infants is the acknowledgment that before we are able to do much of anything, or in any form say "yes" to God, or express any kind of faith, God who created us has already claimed us as his own simply because we exist. As scripture tells us, we are made in God's image and God's own life is woven into the fabric of our being. God knows us before we know God. Though we think our capacity to love originates with us, as we are told in the First Letter of John, we love "because God first loved us."

In spite of the fact that the convivial assembly thought of this as a holiday social event, something very profound happened to me when I was "marked as Christ's own forever," and all that has followed through the various seasons and turnings, the stops, the starts, the detours, has been my continuing struggle to catch up with what occurred that New Year's Day. It amuses me to think that if Christ could use a wedding reception at Cana in Galilee for his first miracle of turning water into wine, a cocktail party could do quite nicely for a baptism.

And So It Begins

St. Augustine of Hippo (354–430) in a baptismal homily instructs the newly baptized to "become what you are not yet." He foresees a lifelong process of growth and discovery as we come to maturity and "grow up in all ways into Christ." We do this not alone, but in communion and fellowship with others. While we might notice changes within ourselves, such as a more compassionate and less judging spirit, it is often people close to us who reveal to us ways we have changed. A spouse, for example, might observe: "You are more patient than you used to be."

Again and again life, as it presents itself, can undo the identities we have forged over the years and we find ourselves bereft of a clear sense of who we are. At such times we try desperately to fix things and restore some sense of order when, in fact, it is only through patience and endurance that the authentic self we are called to become can emerge, not as accomplishment, but as gift. Baptism is the acknowledgment that our lives are not our own but are a gift we hold in trust from the Giver whose Spirit is constantly at work within us—shaping and molding us, transforming and unifying the disparate elements of our humanity.

And so it was with Jesus at his baptism. As he descended into the waters of the Jordan he yielded himself to whatever might lie ahead and to what God would reveal. As he emerged from the river the Spirit bore down upon him and he heard the words:

You are my Son, the Beloved, and with you I am well pleased. (Mark 1:11) His understanding of what this declaration of belovedness would require slowly emerged through the day-by-day living of his life, open and available to the world around him and the men and women he encountered along the way.

It is true that we can choose not to be who God created us to be. We can choose to misuse the gift of our creation in a variety of ways. We can choose to be unloving, hostile, destructive. We humans have ever done so. Therefore, the dramatic language associated with baptism of dying and rising, being reborn, of declaring that if anyone is in Christ there is a new creation, is a way of underscoring the overwhelming consequences of the mystery of our identity . . . being given by God . . . being given back to God . . . as we become who God is calling us to be.

———————

We seek God because God has already found us.
—St. Augustine of Hippo

The first encounter I remember with what I later understood to be the One who had already found me came when I was five. Each afternoon, weather permitting, Mlle. Grassé, a French woman who looked after us, took my younger brother, Stephen, and me for a walk. Our pattern was to walk down the road from our house to a circular driveway in front of an Episcopal church. This half-mile foray seemed like an adventure to Stephen and me. Before returning home we would go into the church's driveway to have our snack of orange juice and graham crackers, our prize for having successfully completed the walk to that turning point without inordinate fussing.

One afternoon I noticed that the gray gothic structure beside the driveway had bright red doors, which beckoned unto me! So I broke free, ran to the doors, and tugged one open. I found myself standing in a hallway filled with dim and mysterious light coming from the stained-glass windows in the church beyond. I realize now that I must have been in the choir vesting area. Black and white garments were hanging from hooks on both sides of the hallway. I remember being overwhelmed by what I would now call the numinous—a sense of mystery that surrounded and fascinated me. At that moment Mlle. Grassé rushed in, pulled me outside, slammed the door, shook her finger at me, and said, "Don't ever go in there again! It's a church!" Little did I realize the irony of that prohibition, given what was yet to come.

"We seek God because God has already found us," as St. Augustine has it. I knew nothing at all about what any of this meant. Standing in that luminous darkness, I did not realize this was an encounter, albeit suitably veiled for my five-year-old capacity to comprehend, which would lead me forward in ways yet to be revealed. There are so many moments in our lives which, as we experience them, seem to have little meaning or consequence. And yet, when we stand back and reflect upon the way we have come thus far we can often see that, when taken together, these seemingly random and sometimes very odd, unsettling occurrences and encounters have brought us to the present moment. They have shaped us and made us who we are. And now, we take a deep breath and turn our face to what may lie ahead.

Consider the work of God; who can make straight what he has made crooked. —Ecclesiastes 7:13

The next year, in the first grade, I was a member of the rat chorus in an operetta version of *The Pied Piper of Hamlin*. Not only was I *in* the rat chorus, I was the *chief* rat, which meant I was to wear a white rat costume while all my fellow rats wore gray. My starring role called for me to stand in front of a semicircle of gray rats and lead them in an exuberant *Rat Dance*. During the dress rehearsal I was overcome with stage fright and refused to do it. The teacher tried to encourage me, but I held firm. Another boy about my size was put into the white rat costume, and I was put into his gray rat costume. The next day at the performance I faded into the background as an indistinguishable member of the chorus. I had given in to fear. As I watched my friend lead the dance I was overcome by regret at the decision I had made.

Even all these years later, I remember saying to myself, "I will never again say 'no' to something out of fear."

Little did I realize at the time that this declaration might have been God's way of opening me beyond the realm of anxiety and fear into what might be God's own purpose. From the distance of these years, there seems to be a clear connection between the white rat and the various situations into which I have been called as priest and bishop, each with its own distinctive costume. All this says to me that God often moves not in straight lines but crooked ones, and that seemingly random events may serve a deeper purpose and prepare us for what is yet to come.

I was following in the footsteps of my father and my mother's father when, at age thirteen, I was sent off to St. Paul's School. The day new boys arrived they were required to audition for the choir, whether or not they wanted to be in the choir. If you could carry a tune you became a chorister, as I did. And now I found myself wearing the black and white garments I had seen hanging on hooks the day I tugged open the red door.

The school chapel is a vast and soaring gothic building. Above the altar is a reredos, an elaborately carved wooden structure populated by statues of saints surrounding gold-trimmed panels depicting the life of Christ. As a member of the choir I was learning to sing liturgical texts with unfamiliar names—*Kyrie, Gloria, Sanctus,* and *Agnus Dei*—as well as hymns and anthems, the likes of which I had never heard before. We were schooled in processing and bowing and quietly finding our places in prayer books and hymnals as the liturgy progressed. I was fascinated by the transcendence of it all, and the solemnity of the worship slowly drew me in. It has been said that students often have to rebel against the culture into which they were born. Since I had no prior church experience, beyond my baptism in accordance with my family's cultural Anglicanism, my rebellion was the opposite. Much to the horror of my family, I seemed to be taking religion far too seriously.

Most of us at the school came from Episcopal roots so it was customary for eighth graders (known in the vocabulary of an

English public school as Second Formers) who had not been confirmed to be part of a confirmation class. Confirmation, a sacramental rite in the Episcopal Church, reaffirms one's baptismal promises and includes a solemn blessing from a bishop. Out of an adolescent sense of orneriness, I said no, I did not want to be confirmed. As it turned out, I was confirmed the following year in a much smaller class of ninth graders. However, I missed most of the confirmation instruction because I was busy building sets for a Molière play. I suspect the priest instructing us did not want to see me yet again the next year, so he simply passed me on to the bishop's hands. I now attribute my decision to be confirmed to "prevenient grace." That is, we may assume our impulse to seek God originates with us when, in fact, we are responding to God's grace which has already gone before us, found us, and laid claim to us.

During my years at St. Paul's I learned that the Episcopal Church makes room for a wide variety of theological opinions and practices, including styles of worship. While some Episcopal churches, often called "low church," prefer simplicity, others, known as "high church," or Anglo-Catholic, are unrestrained in their ceremonial splendor. Not for nothing are the latter remarked on for their "smells and bells"—that is, for their vaporous clouds of incense and elaborate ritual.

On the day we were confirmed the priest who prepared us (who was of the high church persuasion) gave each of us a copy of a little book called *In God's Presence*. It was a mildly Anglo-Catholic devotional manual that contained the order for the Eucharist set out in full with additional prayers to be used to improve upon the celebration privately should the priest have an unfortunate lack of high church sensibilities. It also included morning and evening prayers, various intercessions, and a form for making one's confession in the presence of a priest, a notion I found fascinating. I promptly went to one of the clergy and said I wished to make my confession. Later I learned that news of my request had made its way to the board of trustees, some of whom became concerned that religious enthusiasm might be breaking loose in this school where, for many, good sportsmanship was the established religion.

As part of my newly articulated faith, I joined a fellowship for young high church Episcopalians called the Servants of Christ the King. Membership included a rule of life, with prayers to be said daily and an annual report to be made to a priest designated as "The Director." All of this was perfectly suited to both my adolescent exuberance and my enthusiastic embrace of what was "different." On a deeper level it provided a pattern of discipline and practice that gave shape and direction to my less-than-fully-formed longings toward God. At the time, without being consciously aware of it, I was being slowly drawn deeper into the realm of faith.

———

One of my good friends at St. Paul's came from Manhattan. Tom and his family attended the Church of St. Mary the Virgin, on West 46th Street, known as the citadel and exemplar of all things Catholic in the Anglican tradition. So discreet was St. Mary's about its Episcopal identity that there were notices in the confessionals for the benefit of Roman Catholics who might have mistaken St. Mary's for one of their own churches: *This Is Not a Roman Catholic Church*. I always thought: what a hideous moment to be confronted by that declaration if you were on the verge of pouring out your sins and seeking absolution. I should say parenthetically that St. Mary's is no longer in any way ambiguous about its identity, and with confidence is advertised to be an Episcopal church. In any event, as a young boy Tom had served as an acolyte at St. Mary's and was comfortable with my burgeoning high church sensibilities.

It was the custom on Sundays at St. Paul's for faculty members to invite students to their homes for cider and donuts before the service of Evensong. Accordingly, one Sunday afternoon Tom went off to the home of a priest on the faculty who was at the Anglo-Catholic end of St. Paul's spectrum of churchmanship. He came back to the dorm and greeted me, roaring with laughter. When he stopped laughing enough to get out the words he declared that the teacher had said that I should become a priest! In spite of my religious enthusiasm, which clearly had been noticed, I was stunned. If this notion of my future seemed so bizarre to Tom, maybe I ought to think about it seriously. While many of my classmates spoke of becoming lawyers or bankers like their fathers, I began to speak of wanting to be a priest.

Much as the angel Gabriel surprised and disconcerted Mary by announcing that she was to bear the Son of God, Tom, laughing and pointing at me that long-ago Sunday afternoon, was my angel Gabriel. This, too, was an annunciation; he had announced to me what was to be my future. A seed had been planted and in a way of which I was not fully conscious, I began to turn over in my mind the idea of priesthood.

The popular image of angels is one of chubby cherubs with wings or sweet-faced damsels. However, in scripture angels are messengers in the service of God. They appear in people's lives bearing the news of God's intent. Such messengers have appeared in my life in human form, as friends, colleagues, loved ones, and sometimes as critics. They tend to appear at just the right moment, when I am most in need, even though I don't know it. It is as if they have been sent to tap into some place within me, or my consciousness, to illumine or challenge me or to confirm an intuition.

Inevitably, the priests on the faculty noticed the budding religious enthusiasm of Frank Griswold. One of the priests sent to England for devotional books that were much more advanced than *In God's Presence.* Soon I was reading *The Monastic Diurnal* and studying *Ritual Notes.* It was at this time that I was sent off to Boston for spiritual direction and met Father Pederson. In my senior year I became the head acolyte. I was the terror of the altar guild, and even to some of the clergy, because I would lay down the law as to exactly how things ought to be done. I once overheard the head of the altar guild say to one of its members as I came into view: "Here comes The Last Word!" I think now with a mixture of embarrassment and amusement of that boy who was in the process of becoming who I am today.

—————

I grew up in suburban Philadelphia in what I have noted was a nominally Episcopalian family. My mother had been a devout young girl, and when her beloved father came down with influenza she prayed fervently for his healing. When he died, her faith, unable to withstand this inexplicable loss, died as well.

My father also lost his father to influenza when he was a young boy, leaving him and his sister, Alice, to be raised by their mother and a retinue of nannies and other helpers. My grandmother, also named Alice, was a formidable presence: stern and disapproving of human weakness. I remember her as highly intellectual and fluent in both French and German. Napoleon was her hero and her library held numerous volumes celebrating his life and exploits. Perhaps that might have told me something.

There are bizarre tales of Aunt Alice as a girl which point to a wild and willful nature. When a friend had an appendectomy she was so insistent that she needed one as well that the operation was performed. At one point Grandmother sought to have her committed to a mental institution, and as doctors and orderlies arrived at the house to take her away she screamed for my father to save her. She never forgave him for not being able to do so, though he was a young boy at the time.

In retrospect, I suspect Aunt Alice suffered all her life from some deep psychological disorder that went undiagnosed. Her exploits were fodder for the gossip columns of the day and when she broke a trust it was in all of the papers. She became alienated from my grandmother and eventually moved to London where she led a somewhat reclusive life. Aunt Alice died at her own hand from a drug overdose. She was found lying on her bed with a dog's leash clutched in her hand. Her beloved canine companion had died not long before, perhaps taking with him the all-accepting devotion and love she had never experienced from her family and those around her.

My father's path was also difficult. Sometime in his early years he had a fistfight which horribly bloodied the son of a neighbor and so upset my grandmother that she packed him off to live for a time with an Episcopal clergyman to give him the "discipline" she believed he lacked. The experience was traumatic and left him suspicious and fearful of anything related to the church. When he later went off to St. Paul's, the religious life of the school was not the consolation for him that it was for me. Though he dropped out of Harvard after his freshman year, most likely because of lack of interest, he had a keen mind and read widely and deeply. He possessed a natural aptitude for all things mechanical and established a company that manufactured precision measuring equipment. He had a passion for auto racing and indeed was the winner of the first Watkins Glen Grande Prix in 1948.

My father had been an alcoholic for as long as I can remember and ultimately died of the disease at age fifty-four, when I was thirty-one. By that time he was estranged from my mother, who had remarried, and was living on his own. Decades after his death, I learned through a curious sequence of circumstances that the priest he had been sent to live with for "discipline" quite likely had been a pedophile, though he had gone to his grave before this was revealed. I think now about what my father might have experienced as a vulnerable young boy, and how it might have contributed to his alcoholism and fear of the church. I will never know.

My religious enthusiasm was difficult enough for my father, so my desire to be ordained terrified him. As for my mother, when I announced that I would need to go to church each Sunday when I was home from St. Paul's, she then shared with me the story of how her faith had been dormant since the death of her father. She told me that as a child she had gone to church regularly and it had been very important for her.

After I made my announcement, Mother conferred with some friends who told her they thought highly of the Rev. Dr. Thorne Sparkman, the rector of the Church of the Redeemer in Bryn Mawr, Pennsylvania, and urged her to go there. As I was too young to have a driver's license, Mother drove me to church each Sunday. As it turned out, my own developing faith was the key for her in reawakening her own.

Dr. Sparkman was from South Carolina, a learned man who had been a Rhodes Scholar at Oxford, and an old-fashioned southern high churchman who held a high doctrine of the church and its sacramental life while eschewing the ceremonial extravagances associated with the Anglo-Catholic tradition.

When I was home on school vacations I continued to be an acolyte at the Church of the Redeemer and Dr. Sparkman became an important mentor to me during those school years.

Once I asked him to hear my confession. When I told my mother what I was about to do she said: "Darling, what will he think of you?" I replied that he would think I was a sinner—just like him.

———

After St. Paul's, and again following in my father's path, I entered Harvard College where I majored in English and French Literature. Being in Cambridge, and just blocks away from the monastery of the Society of Saint John the Evangelist, was a happy circumstance for me. During my four years as an undergraduate I was a frequent acolyte at the monastery and served at the Eucharist several times each week and at Sunday Vespers, followed by the Benediction of the Blessed Sacrament.

Being an acolyte at the monastery meant being open to surprise. All sorts and conditions of humanity found their way in and out of the chapel. One weekday as I came in with the priest to the Lady Chapel where the nine o'clock morning mass was celebrated, I noticed that none other than T.S. Eliot was in the congregation. I have to confess that his presence was quite a distraction, and as I moved the missal and rang the bell I kept wondering if he noticed me. I hoped he was the kind of Episcopalian who stays until the candles are extinguished so I would have the opportunity of imposing myself upon him. Alas. Very wisely he slipped out the moment the priest and I left the altar and was well gone by the time I returned to perform the candle extinguishing. I guess Mr. Eliot had had enough of the people who wanted to importune him while he was trying to worship.

I vividly remember one middle-aged woman who frequented the chapel. She also came from Philadelphia and I knew her slightly as our families had some association. Perhaps because of her wealth she passed for eccentric rather than simply crazy. And, because any damage caused by her various eccentricities could always be paid for, no one put a brake on her frequently peculiar behavior. She normally sat in the back of the chapel during one of the weekday masses reading the *New York Times* and was not shy in shouting out for the benefit of the priest at the altar: "I can't hear a word!" I note here that in those days the preferred way of presiding for many Anglo-Catholic clergy was with a monotone mumble approximating rapidly read Latin, so her protestations were not altogether out of line.

One day as the community entered the chapel for one of the offices of prayer they noticed that she was suspended from the iron grill that separated the choir from the congregation. Apparently she had tried to climb over it and her coat had gotten caught on several of the spikes. There she hung, flailing about, until rescued by the good fathers.

Equally memorable was the intense Russian woman who accosted me one day and, pointing at the wilted flowers in front of the statue of Mary, declared: "Father X looked at them and killed them. He is possessed by Satan, you do know!" Unbeknownst to me, such experiences were preparing me for some of the sorts and conditions of humanity I was to meet as priest and bishop.

Perhaps a counterbalance to the intensity of my involvement in the ongoing liturgical life of the monastery was my equal investment of time and energy in the life of the *Harvard Lampoon*, an undergraduate humor magazine that, as the name suggests, pokes fun in its pages at the foibles and failures of humanity and venerable institutions at Harvard and beyond. The magazine occupies a wonderfully eccentric building, commonly known as the Lampoon Castle, situated on a small island of land in the middle of Mt. Auburn Street.

As part of my initiation to the *Lampoon* staff, I was told I had to make curtains for all of the windows and was presented with a sewing machine, a device previously unknown to me. Each curtain consisted of a blue and yellow panel that I was meant to sew together. Somehow I did it, and for years after my graduation I walked by the building to see if my curtains were still hanging. They endured for quite a long time, a memorial to my late-night labors.

I particularly remember my contributions to the magazine's Religious Revival issue and the issue satirizing literary *erotica*. My story for the latter, presumed to have been translated from the French, involved Sensualita who, as the story unfolds, is being led to the *chambre de plaisir*. The tale was building to a lusty conclusion as it reached the bottom of a page, to be continued elsewhere in the magazine. Quite intentionally the continuation page did not exist. Somehow that issue of the *Lampoon* found its way to the monastery and came to the attention of one of the fathers who was shocked and appalled that the pious acolyte engaged in such antics.

Years later, when I was Presiding Bishop, my past came back and reasserted itself when I was the First Runner Up for the *Clement Biddle Wood '47 Award*, Clement Wood having been another *Lampoon* staffer in his Harvard days. In typical *Lampoon* fashion, no one is ever accorded first prize. As First Runner Up, I was presented with a properly engraved champagne bucket at a cocktail party at the home of George Plimpton, who after his time at Harvard and on the staff of the *Lampoon* went on to distinguish himself as a prolific author, editor, actor, and as the founder of *The Paris Review*. Sadly, he had died between the planning of the event and the date it occurred. However, Mrs. Plimpton graciously honored the invitation and the party was held as planned. The evening was a time of grateful remembrance of Plimpton's inquiring mind and exuberant spirit.

Sometime after that I was asked to preside at a service at Memorial Church in Harvard Yard on the anniversary of the *Lampoon's* founding. John Updike was to read a remembrance of George Plimpton, both of them having written for the magazine during their Harvard years. Instead, someone else read a memorial for John Updike who had just died . . . One never knows.

In the summer following my sophomore year I signed up to be part of a work camp sponsored by the Episcopal Church on the Cheyenne River Indian Reservation in South Dakota. I vividly remember flying to Pierre in a suit and necktie only to be greeted by one of the leaders of the work camp in jeans and cowboy boots. He took one look at me, and I am sure he wondered how this overdressed college boy would fare in the badlands of South Dakota.

The experience was overwhelming and obliged me to confront and relinquish many of my cultural assumptions. Though Sunday services were announced for particular times, they actually only began at whatever time the congregation arrived. This seeming inability to abide by clock time was derisively referred to as "Indian time." However, as the summer wore on, the notion that things should take place when people are ready for them to take place was very liberating. It taught me to view time in terms of people and their natural rhythms of life rather than the unforgiving movements of a clock.

The reservation stores were overseen by Anglos rather than members of the tribe because, in the native culture, if someone came into a shop needing something and was unable to pay for it, ties of kinship overrode the profit motive and what was needed was freely given. This was another lesson for me, this time about generosity.

By the end of the summer I had cast aside the suit and tie in which I had arrived, and along with them many of my unexamined assumptions. I bought boots, a black cowboy hat, and grew a beard.

———

Here am I; send me! —Isaiah 6:8

During my college years, without my being fully aware of it, I was being subtly sorted and sifted through the repeated rhythms of sacrament and prayer. It became ever clearer to me that the path I was called to follow, and through which I was to live out the implications of my baptism, was ordination to the priesthood. I was discovering that having been sealed with the sign of the cross on that January day in 1938 was an omen of things yet to come.

As my sense of vocation grew over time, I was surprised and unsettled. I needed to test my intuition and ask myself what was calling to me. Was it my own ego? Or, was it God's Spirit? Was I to declare "I am called," or rather to frame it as a question—"Am I called?"—a question to be explored with the help of others? Did others consider my sense of call authentic and congruent with the person they knew me to be? In ways more casual than intentional, I was testing my sense of call against the wisdom and insights proffered by close friends and clergy, particularly Dr. Sparkman.

After this period of questioning a moment of clarity arrived and I knew the time had come for me formally to acknowledge my sense of call. At that time, the route to ordination lay almost exclusively in the hands of the bishop. Oliver J. Hart, the then Bishop of Pennsylvania, gave his approval for me to proceed to seminary after my graduation from college. My interview with Bishop Hart took an unexpected turn when he told me that prior to our meeting he had been summoned by my grandmother, who told him in no uncertain terms that my entrance into the ordained ministry would be nothing less than "an unconscionable waste of a fine education." Grandmother regarded clergy as something of a cultural necessity. One would turn to a clergyman to perform certain ceremonies at stated moments requiring a public ritual observed in the name of God, namely baptisms, weddings, and funerals. This was often expressed more humorously as the need one had for clergy in order to be "hatched, matched, and dispatched."

Upon the recommendation of several college friends who were also pursuing ordination, I applied to The General Theological Seminary in New York, a venerable institution and the only official seminary of the Episcopal Church. As its title implies, General sought to represent the theological and liturgical breadth of the Episcopal Church, though clearly it came down on the high church side of the spectrum.

During my first year at General a fellow seminarian who had recently returned from studying theology at Oxford spoke appreciatively of the experience and urged me and another seminarian to consider a similar course. His suggestion deeply resounded within me for a number of reasons. That the Society of Saint John the Evangelist looked to England, and more specifically Oxford, as the place of its origin was certainly a factor, as was Dr. Sparkman's connection with Oxford. As well, the plethora of devotional books and manuals of prayer and ritual I had been absorbing since my St. Paul's days had the imprint of the Church of England. All of this made me eager to drink deep from the source of Anglicanism. Accordingly, my friend and I applied to Oriel College, Oxford, and both of us were accepted for the following year.

Soon after I arrived at Oxford my romantic notions were challenged by reality. The similarity of language had lulled me into thinking that the rhythms of life in England would also be similar to life in Cambridge. I quickly discovered that the culture of an English university was very different from the university culture I had known in the United States. This showed itself, among other things, in the food where a meal of steak and kidney pie and two kinds of potatoes was typical dining hall fare. Vegetables were not to be seen. Though this was trivial in one way, it was a metaphor for all of the differences I felt, now separated from family and friends and the ordinary details of the life I had taken for granted at home. I was unmoored from the familiar and searching for my own grounding.

There was, of course, no email or Skype or any of the other ways we now communicate instantaneously around the world. Even the idea of a trans-Atlantic telephone call seemed extravagant. I maintained my contact with home through a weekly exchange of letters with Mother and occasionally with Grandmother, who had taken on the expense of my Oxford years.

I knew my Aunt Alice was living in London, though estranged from the family, and I decided to seek her out, thinking she might look kindly on her nephew. Though she no longer lived at the address my grandmother had given me, I found her with the help of an estate agent and appeared unannounced at her door. She received me politely and offered me a cup of tea. Then in the week that followed I received a letter from her saying that under no circumstances would she see me again. Perhaps I should not have been surprised, knowing what I did of her history. And thus the door was closed on what I had hoped would be a familial connection while far from home.

In the university setting of Oxford, the Church of England was revealed in all of its breadth and contradictions. Though the official liturgy was that of the 1662 Book of Common Prayer, seldom did you find it celebrated without some "enrichments" from other sources, Roman Catholic or otherwise. The tensions of the Reformation were still very much present and unresolved as well. Though I was familiar with the breadth of opinion and practice within the Episcopal Church in the United States, the extremes of the Church of England seemed more pronounced than those in the Episcopal Church at home. While one congregation used the Roman Missal in Latin, another celebrated the Eucharist only infrequently and on a plain wooden table devoid of any ornaments such as candles or cross. Yet, both were *bona fide* congregations of the Church of England, the "Established Church" of the land. The extremes left me feeling unsettled and it was hard for me to find anything that reminded me of the more stable liturgy I had grown accustomed to at home.

In my state of spiritual loneliness, my confessor, a compassionate and large-hearted retired priest who lived in a boarding house not far from the church where he regularly celebrated the Eucharist, was a great consolation. From time to time he would invite me for tea and on such occasions his kindly and hospitable landlady would set out a plate of cakes and insist that, "as a growing boy," I must eat them all. More than a spiritual guide, he became for me a wise and loving father. He did not so much trouble himself with my sins as he did with my loneliness. He always addressed me as "My dear boy," and just that "My dear boy" was an incredible gift to me. As I now "track down the Holy Ghost" and seek to follow the lines of spiritual motion, I realize that his voice was truly a gift of the Spirit.

My course of study involved the preparation of a weekly essay for my tutor who would assign a topic and then recommend what I should read in order to prepare it. His recommendations were made in a particularly understated way. "You might want to look into so-and-so's book on such-and-such," actually meant "you had better read it carefully." Often the recommended readings included diametrically opposed points of view and the task was to draw profit from both perspectives and bring them together in an essay of graceful reasonableness. This was an invitation to find the gray area between the black and white of the more extreme positions. As is clear to me now, this was an expression of classical Anglicanism and the via media, the middle way, arrived at not by compromise but rather through synthesis.

While I took my theological studies seriously, I was not reluctant to put the books aside, leaving Moses on Mount Sinai. When we were able to acquire a car, a friend and I would ramble through the English countryside. On one such outing we noticed a road sign with an arrow pointing toward Little Gidding. Except for T.S. Eliot's "Fourth Quartet," so named, I had no idea what Little Gidding might be. Our curiosity piqued, we followed the arrow and discovered, exactly as Eliot had described it, a small church in front of which lay the tomb of Nicholas Ferrar. We entered the church and found a pamphlet that explained how in the seventeenth century Ferrar had established a community in a nearby manor house. It was made up of members of his family who followed a rigorous rule of worship based on the services provided in the Book of Common Prayer. Reading further, I discovered that Ferrar and the priest/poet George Herbert were friends, and that Herbert, as he was dying, bequeathed his poetry to Ferrar, telling him to do with it as he chose. Thus, through my "accidental" finding of Little Gidding I was led to George Herbert and later sought out Bemerton, near Salisbury, where Herbert served as rector and ordered his life and that of his congregation according to the rhythms and seasons of the Prayer Book.

On another occasion I stopped in the hamlet of Pusey where the surplice that had once been worn by the great nineteenth-century apostle of the Oxford Movement, Edward Bouverie Pusey, was enshrined in a glass case. Through these and similar excursions, I came to know something of the saints of the

Church of England and the central place worship occupied in their lives.

Oxford had six-week vacation periods between terms. Commercial trans-Atlantic flights were costly and returning home by ship was both impractical and expensive. These vacation periods were designed to give students a time for further reading and study. I saw these as splendid opportunities to visit the Continent, particularly Paris, where a college classmate was studying music.

During one of these sojourns I sought out the Church of Saint-Séverin on the Left Bank, the most progressive parish in Paris in those days. Saint-Séverin was at the forefront of the Liturgical Movement, which aimed to render the classical patterns of Christian worship in forms that were accessible and intelligible to contemporary worshipers. The liturgical movement, born in the Benedictine monasteries of Europe in the late nineteenth and early twentieth centuries, sought to return to the sources out of which the formal worship of the church had evolved. The primary motivation of the liturgical movement was to deepen and expand people's encounter with the Lord in word and sacrament. It aimed to recover the intrinsic power of sign, symbol, and scripture to reveal the living Christ in the midst of, and within, those gathered for worship.

My awareness of the power of liturgy to speak to the heart in a language of sign and symbol had been awakened at St. Paul's when I was the terror of the altar guild. Now, during my years at Oxford, it was strengthened by my encounters with the legacies of Nicholas Ferrar and George Herbert, who ordered their lives in accordance with the liturgy of the Book of Common Prayer. It was further expanded by the experiences at Saint-Séverin and elsewhere on the Continent, including the Benedictine Abbey of Saint-André in Bruges, Belgium. Through these experiences, my eyes were being opened to a whole new vision of how the Eucharist and other rites might be celebrated in a way that made them more transparent to the needs and sensibilities of an engaged and active congregation.

According to long-standing Oxford tradition, a "University Sermon" is delivered each Sunday, usually in the University Church of St. Mary the Virgin. Several years ago I was invited to be the preacher. As it was the Sunday closest to the Feast of the Nativity of John the Baptist, the sermon was to be preached from the outdoor pulpit in the courtyard of Magdalen College. During the Middle Ages Magdalen had absorbed a hospital under the patronage of John the Baptist, and one of the conditions of the merger was that a sermon be preached annually in his honor. With the wind whipping about me I stood in the pulpit, firmly gripping the fluttering sheets of my sermon notes. In that moment I realized that never in the wildest imaginings of my student days could I have foreseen becoming a bishop and one day being invited to preach the University Sermon.

Indeed, God is the God of constant, often disconcerting, surprises. What we shall be has yet to be revealed, as the First Letter of John tells us, and what we shall be is an amalgam of the various bits and pieces, starts and stops, circuitous routes and moments of losing and finding that become avenues to discovering dimensions of ourselves we had never imagined were part of who God is calling us to be.

—————

Your vocation is that place where your deep gladness meets
the world's great hunger.　　　—Frederick Buechner

My ordination as a deacon on the morning of December 2, 1962, at Christ Church in Pottstown, Pennsylvania, was a significant milepost on my journey. The assistant at the church was to be ordained to the priesthood that day and, because a bishop was going to be available, as is required to do the deed, my ordination was squeezed into the occasion. I had been called as a curate at the Church of the Redeemer in Bryn Mawr, Pennsylvania, the parish that had sponsored me for ordination, and Dr. Sparkman was eager for me to be ordained and begin my formal ministry by Christmas.

I arose early that morning in a state of expectation, and put on my newly purchased clerical collar—part of the uniform for what would be my new life. Of course, I checked in the mirror and saw an unruly tuft of hair quite unbefitting the dignity of a new deacon. When water would not tame it, I found my mother's hair spray and went to work. Never having used such a product, I didn't realize that aiming the spray at my face was a very bad idea. It stung, and my eyes turned so red that I arrived at the church looking as if I might have spent the morning weeping, overcome by anticipatory emotion.

The ordaining bishop was the Rt. Rev. Andrew Y.Y. Tsu, who was then serving as an assisting bishop in the Diocese of Pennsylvania. Bishop Tsu had an impressive history, having been consecrated in Shanghai in 1940 as the eighth Chinese Anglican bishop. During World War II he became known as "the Bishop of the Burma Road" because of his care for Allied troops as they made their way on the international highway that cut through his district. In 1949 he fled to the United States before the Communist advance. His time in Pennsylvania was presumably less hazardous.

As it happened on that December morning, the service moved along through the ordinations to the Eucharist, at which point Bishop Tsu sank into a chair and asked the new priest to take over, surprising us all. We made it through, and after the service he told us that he was in great pain, having fallen on the ice that morning while getting into his car. After the service he was whisked off to the hospital where he discovered that he had broken his hip. He had bravely endured excruciating pain rather than halt the proceedings and disappoint the ordinands. This seemed an inauspicious beginning to the ordained life and perhaps should have signaled me to be alert for unexpected twists and turns that lay ahead.

During my time as Presiding Bishop I visited China and met with Bishop K.H. Ting, who was then ninety years old and the last remaining Chinese Anglican bishop. I was pleased to be able to tell him that Bishop Tsu, whom he had known, had ordained me. Bishop Ting was delighted to know the church in China was part of my "ecclesial DNA."

A new chapter had begun, and I was ready to take my place at the Church of the Redeemer. My first day I sat behind a large and well-polished wooden desk in an office all my own, feeling all the authority and confidence of a new deacon. Then the parish secretary appeared in the doorway and said, "Mr. Griswold, we need you." I was ready for action. Was a parishioner who had just lost a loved one waiting to see me? Had someone suffered a horrible accident so I should rush to the hospital? I was ready to do what needed to be done. "Mr. Griswold, we are getting ready for Sunday school. Could you please sharpen these pencils?" My heart sank. As I contemplated the boxes of No. 2 pencils, I wondered if this was what it was all about. In retrospect, that was an important moment. Most certainly, in the years that have followed, the equivalent of pencil sharpening has been required over and over again. On that morning I took a first step toward realizing that drudgery can indeed be "divine" if done for God, as George Herbert prays in his poem "The Elixir."

> Teach me, my God and King,
> In all things thee to see,
> And what I do in any thing,
> To do it as for thee . . .

Dr. Sparkman's influence on me became more pronounced, now that I was on his staff. He was a man of few words and led largely by indirection. Seldom did he ask me to do something or comment on the way I exercised my ministry. I soon realized that his seeming disregard masked an incredible attentiveness. Nothing passed him by. Because he rarely offered a suggestion, when he did I took it with full seriousness. He was exactly what my youthful spirit needed.

He led a very disciplined life and, unlike many rectors of large, multi-staff parishes who might have delegated the early Eucharist on Sunday to one of the assistants, he was always present, even if he only assisted in distributing communion. I remember once visiting him while he was hospitalized during a brief illness. As I entered the room he quickly slid his Prayer

Book and Bible under the sheets. I knew exactly what he had been doing—reading Daily Morning Prayer—and that he was fulfilling Jesus's admonition to "beware of practicing your piety before others."

On one occasion, a Main Line matron accosted him at a cocktail party and said: "Thorne, surely the Episcopal Church doesn't have confession!" In his usual direct manner he simply replied, "It most certainly does." And that was the end of that.

Perhaps the most significant role Dr. Sparkman played in my life was as a grandfather. When his son and daughter-in-law had their first child, one of the godmothers, though I didn't suspect it at the time, was to be my future wife, Phoebe Wetzel, who had been a college classmate of the baby's mother. The rector's daughter-in-law promptly decided that her dear friend and the unmarried curate ought to get together. All sorts of stratagems were put into play but the two of us resisted until the younger Sparkmans left town. The rest, as they say, is history.

On Sunday, June 23, 1963, I was ordained to the priesthood at the Church of the Redeemer. On this occasion Bishop J. Gillespie Armstrong presided without incident. Appropriately, the preacher on that occasion was Father Pederson of the Society of Saint John the Evangelist, who had guided me since I had been sent to him from St. Paul's as an overwrought adolescent.

Reflections on Vocation

Every person's fundamental vocation, according to St. Irenaeus, a second-century Church theologian, is to reflect the glory of God: "For the glory of God is a human person fully alive, and the life of humanity consists in the vision of God." We all share the vocation of living lives that reflect as best we can God's way of being toward the world and humankind: merciful, compassionate, loving, forgiving, just. In this way we become who we are truly called to be. God's glory is revealed as we are brought fully to life by the Spirit—the "giver of life"—working in and through us.

As one of the characters in Gail Godwin's novel *Evensong* observes: "Something is your vocation if it keeps making more of you." True enough, but "being made more of" is not easy and only happens at a cost. For Christians, being made more of involves our participation in Christ's paschal pattern: again and again we experience, in our own lives, death followed by resurrection. The living out of this reality takes place through the whole length of our lives, and is determined in large measure by the events and circumstances that shape and form us. Ordained ministry has been my way of living out this reality, and I continue to reflect on what it means and calls out of me.

I naively assumed that my being called to ordained ministry meant God recognized my competence and my ordination was its acknowledgment. Only after some very painful encounters *with* my limitations did I realize the call was not about my competency at all. I was being called *with* my limitations and inadequacies—my "thorns" intact, to borrow from St. Paul—and the journey that began with my ordination would lead to the recognition of both my imperfections and gifts I didn't know I possessed. Through this I have been given to know something of God's boundless compassion and God's capacity to embrace all that I am.

Cardinal Mercier, Primate of the Roman Catholic Church in Belgium early in the last century, once told a group of seminarians that if God called them to the ordained ministry it was because they could not be trusted to live out the implications of their baptism as laypersons. Perhaps God knows we need more, and the grace bestowed in ordination is an invitation to journey into the deep mystery of one's selfhood, not as we might wish to construct it but as it exists in the mind and heart and imagination of God.

"For me, priesthood means speaking with a full voice." So said Alexander Elchaninov in *The Diary of a Russian Priest*. Father Elchaninov (1891–1934), a Russian Orthodox priest, was ordained in France after the Russian Revolution. I sense in his words that, for him, being a priest was a doorway to a deeper discovery of who he was and was called to be in the love and mercy of God.

In 1967, after almost four years of serving as Dr. Sparkman's assistant, I was called to be rector of St. Andrew's Church in Yardley, Pennsylvania, across the Delaware River from Trenton, New Jersey. Our move to Yardley merited coverage in *The Trenton Times*. The big news was not about the rector but rather the rector's wife. As it happens, Phoebe's grandfather was Dr. William Wetzel, a former principal of Trenton High School. He was best remembered for having thrown a hymnbook at a bat during a school assembly, instantly felling it. And thus the focus of the local newspaper story was: *Trenton girl returns home.*

When Phoebe and I moved from Bryn Mawr to Yardley, within a year of our marriage, Yardley was still a quiet country town. St. Andrew's rectory was a large and comfortable house directly across the street from the church. The church building, picturesquely situated on the banks of an eighteenth-century millpond, was first erected in 1827 as a simple stone building resembling a meetinghouse. Then, in 1889, in the wake of the Gothic revival, the church was remodeled. The clear glass of the meetinghouse was replaced by stained glass and the building was generally "gothicized."

Though Yardley is only an hour away from Bryn Mawr, the changes were huge. For one, I was the sole priest and the staff consisted of a volunteer part-time secretary. She was the wife of the local obstetrician who, in due course, delivered our daughters, Hannah and Eliza. Also, the contrast between a church that easily seated at least 600 and one that seated at most 120 was reflected in a far more intimate liturgical style in Yardley. Even at a slow pace, a procession down the aisle in Yardley took approximately 20 seconds, which precluded any of the pomp that was possible processing down the long aisle in Bryn Mawr.

In addition, St. Andrew's congregation was far more diverse, made up as it was of families who had lived in Yardley and its environs for many years, and a changing group of people who commuted daily to New York by train from nearby Trenton, and who were frequently transferred in and out of the community. As the wife of one such person said to me, "You'd better go meet your next-door neighbor as soon as they move in because if you wait they may be gone."

The ritual patterns, symbolic actions, and even the gestures of the priest during worship can take us beyond the realm of words and become a means of proclaiming the gospel and fostering an encounter with Christ. A rector in an Episcopal church is in charge of worship; now, no longer constrained by the patterns of worship at the Church of the Redeemer, I was free to instigate many of the changes inspired by the Liturgical Movement I had experienced in full force in England and in France while I was at Oxford. The power of liturgy to shape and inform had taken deep root within me during those years, and I was eager to share with my congregation what had become so life-giving to me. St. Andrew's became a laboratory for the experimental liturgies that were then being authorized for trial use throughout the Episcopal Church. For example, I promptly pulled the altar away from the back wall so I could face the people. The reaction to my innovations was varied. While some parishioners bemoaned the loss of the comfortably familiar, others welcomed the changes. In addition, new faces appeared, drawn by what they felt was progressive energy.

In all of this music played an important role. Along the way, I joined forces with a local musician, Dick Averre, who played the piano on Saturday nights at a restaurant in nearby New Hope owned by Juanita Hall, the singer and actress who played the original Bloody Mary in *South Pacific.* After his restaurant gig on Saturday nights Dick took his place at the organ on Sunday mornings. As new directions in liturgy unfolded, his talent as a composer, and the ease with which he employed instruments other than the organ, further enriched our liturgical life.

Dick and I worked well together and from time to time I would sit down in his living room and hand him something I had written that he would then set to music. When we sensed a certain rightness Dick would call in his wife, Marcia, to sing the fruit of our collaboration while he played the accompaniment. This process was often helped along by a bit of gin, which on occasion dulled our critical faculties. The following Sunday we would try out what we had created with the congregation. Some of our efforts have been published and continue to be used, while others, mercifully, have disappeared.

While Dr. Sparkman had given me a great deal of freedom and responsibility, and had on occasion accepted some of my ideas, he remained very much in charge. Therefore, I arrived at St. Andrew's with little experience in leadership. Being a rector required a whole new set of skills. I realize now how much I was formed by the congregation. Through their patience and wise counsel, not to mention occasional criticism, they drew forth from me abilities and a capacity for leadership I did not know I possessed. They could also be immensely compassionate and forgiving when my creativity got out of hand. I began to understand, sometimes reluctantly and not without pain, that Christ calls us forth, encourages us, and challenges us through the limbs and members of his body, which I encountered in the multiplicity of personalities represented by the congregation. It was at St. Andrew's that I began to find my "full voice" as a priest.

As is the case with many priests and pastors I have known, the congregation was my reality—my little world. Though I knew intellectually that the diocese with its bishop, rather than the congregation, is the basic unit of the Episcopal Church, I felt somewhat removed from the Diocese of Pennsylvania, which has its offices in Philadelphia. In part this was because most of the congregation thought of New York or Trenton, rather than Philadelphia, as their urban focus. I must confess that, for the most part, I ignored the diocese. All of this was about to change.

As I emerged from a church in Philadelphia one day after what I thought was a particularly lifeless diocesan liturgy, I complained to a brother priest, "That was about the dreariest service I've ever been through." I then felt a tap on my shoulder and turned to see Robert L. DeWitt, my bishop, who had presided at the service, smiling benignly. He said, "Well, if that's the way you feel, would you please plan the next liturgy for the diocese?" Flushed with embarrassment at being overheard, I awkwardly accepted his invitation with appropriate enthusiasm, and mixed feelings. Suddenly I found myself in the enlarged world of diocesan responsibility for matters liturgical. This occurred in the 1960s, in the height of the era of oddly confected vestments in unusual colors bedecked with felt cutouts held on by Stitch-Witchery. It was the season of guitars and drums and when we belted out "We Are One in the Spirit" and sang "they'll know we are Christians by our love," it was all still fresh and new. My chance comment, surprisingly overheard, had driven me unwittingly into the center of the liturgical life of the diocese such that I now planned all diocesan liturgies, even to the point of designing, at his sufferance, Bishop DeWitt's miter. God's ironic sense of humor was much in evidence.

Looking back, I see now that my years at St. Andrew's were rich in blessings and broadened my perspective, carrying me beyond the familiar and somewhat circumscribed borders of my Main Line Philadelphia upbringing. After seven years I was called from Yardley to the Church of St. Martin in the Fields in the Chestnut Hill neighborhood of Philadelphia.

When, in 1974, we made our move to St. Martin's, Phoebe, in virtue of her own history, had once again prepared the way. Up through high school she attended Springside School, which was a short walk from St. Martin's, and once acted in the role of a French policeman in a school play performed on the stage of the parish house.

In many ways, St. Martin's was similar to the Church of the Redeemer. As it happened, some older members of the congregation knew, or had known, my parents and grandparents. On my first Sunday I was greeted by a large congregation eager to see who the vestry had chosen as their new rector. For my part, I was equally curious about them. I decided that rather than launching directly into the liturgy for the day I should first introduce myself and give the congregation some sense of the parish from which I had come. While many of those present were familiar with the Church of the Redeemer in Bryn Mawr, very few had any idea where Yardley was, let alone St. Andrew's. With all this in mind I decided to wear a patchwork vestment that had been lovingly made and presented to me on my last Sunday in Yardley. Each patch, all in various shades of orange, represented a particular person or family. "I come among you with a past and a history," I said to my new congregation. I explained that the vestment meant a great deal to me, symbolizing as it did the reality of all our lives being stitched together in Christ. Then, as I extended my arms to reveal the vestment's full glory, some members of the congregation, accustomed to the usual liturgical colors, gasped audibly. Needless to say, orange is not one of them, a point that was not lost on certain members of the altar guild sitting in the congregation.

Unlike St. Andrew's, St. Martin's was accustomed to a full-time staff which, in addition to the rector, included an assistant priest, a sexton, an organist/choirmaster, and a parish secretary. Also, unlike St. Andrew's, St. Martin's was a far more settled congregation and in many ways possessed of a stronger sense of tradition and "how things ought to be."

My arrival at St. Martin's coincided with the Episcopal Church's continuing season of experimentation with a variety of liturgical forms leading to the revision of its Prayer Book, which had not been revised since 1928. *"Lex orandi, lex credendi:* The law of praying is the law of believing." This ancient saying captures something of the place the Book of Common Prayer has traditionally occupied in the life of the Episcopal Church. Because the faith of the church is expressed in its liturgical forms and language, changes in form and expansion of the language about God can provoke a wide range of reactions, positive and negative. The philosopher Eric Hoffer once observed that change, even when welcomed at the level of the mind, is experienced as loss at a more visceral level. Though we may be able to see the benefits of a change in a familiar pattern, nonetheless, in embracing it we may experience a deep sense of inner disorientation.

Though St. Martin's had not been immune to the Liturgical Movement and the trial rites of the Episcopal Church, not all were ready for the more drastic effects occasioned by my arrival. During a parish meeting when the head of the altar guild, who was possessed of a sly sense of humor, gave her report she solemnly declared that "the purpose of the altar guild is to care for the altar." She then paused, and went on:

"Of course, at St. Martin's we never know where it will *be* on any given Sunday."

"He ought to know better," exclaimed one disconcerted member of the congregation concerning my innovations, while another declared the exchange of the Peace to be "the kiss of death." As the moment drew near he would kneel with an open hymnal over his head to preclude any contact with those around him.

For me the task was not so much a question of external change as it was to help people appropriate the changes at a personal level, and take them in as enhancements to their encounter with God. In time, what may have seemed novel and external became for many an enrichment of their faith and encounter with God through the signs and symbols of the liturgy.

Though clergy are frequently counseled not to establish close friendships with parishioners, Phoebe and I found that our closest friends, both in Yardley and Chestnut Hill, were members of the congregation. Often the bond was established because we had children of the same age who played together. During my years as a parish priest it became ever clearer to me that priest and people are, in some sense, for one another's salvation. The idea of the priest as "the deliverer" of the word and members of the congregation as "the receivers" is profoundly deficient. As in the case of St. Andrew's, and before that the Church of the Redeemer, my time at St. Martin's was an experience of grace and blessing. Again and again I found myself encouraged, challenged, illumined, corrected, convicted, and inspired by members of the congregation who were ministers and word-bearers to me.

———

Three sayings from the Desert Fathers of the fourth century have been important to me in relation to my experience of parish ministry:

"Remain in your cell and your cell will teach you everything."
"Your cell is a furnace."
"Life and death are in the hands of your brother."

Remain in your cell and your cell will teach you everything. This text describes the cell as the place where the monk is most directly exposed to himself before the mystery of God. It is a place of dis-illusion where false notions of self fall away. The same can occur in the life of a pastor within the context of a specific local congregation.

This idea of staying in place echoes St. Benedict's notion of stability; that is, opening ourselves to inner growth mediated by the Spirit who meets us when we are intensely present to where we are. This means avoiding the temptation to look for a "better situation," but rather remaining in place, living in deeper availability to God, who is present where we are, and in the members of the congregation, as problematic and difficult as some of them might be. There are, of course, circumstances when, following the counsel of Jesus, we are called to shake the dust from our shoes and move on. Knowing which is which is a matter for careful discernment.

Your cell is a furnace. This saying uses the image of a furnace whose refining fire rids us of the dross and purifies the essential ore often buried within us. This notion is captured in the words of a well-known hymn, "How Firm a Foundation":

When through fiery trials thy pathways shall lie,
My grace, all sufficient, shall be thy supply;
The flame shall not hurt thee; I only design
Thy dross to consume, and thy gold to refine.

Life and death are in the hands of your brother. It took me some years to recognize that serving in a particular church was not simply an historical accident or the preference of a search committee but rather an invitation to a deeper encounter with God mediated by interaction with the congregation. Life and death are indeed in the hands of those around us. Often, I have prayed or searched the scripture for some enlightening or illumining word, and then, much to my surprise, the word I needed—be it a challenge, a consolation, or an encouragement— came from a human voice: perhaps an intervening angel. We are created to be word-bearers to one another. Over time, the parishioner who protected himself with a hymnal against an exchange of the peace became a friend. Though he did not relinquish his protective hymnal, I came to realize he was a gift: he saved me from thinking that my views on liturgy were the only valid ones. He had uncovered my ego investment in winning everyone over to my point of view.

Though I had never taken much interest in matters of church governance, because of my involvement in the liturgical life of the diocese I was elected as a representative from the Diocese of Pennsylvania to the 1976 General Convention of the Episcopal Church. The General Convention is a bicameral legislative body of bishops, clergy, and lay deputies that meets every three years for a week or more. The 1976 General Convention saw the formal presentation of the Draft Proposed Book of Common Prayer. The debate on the pros and cons of the new book was vigorous. At one point I spoke and declared, "The book is a banquet. Let us keep the feast." To my surprise this sound bite reverberated. One of the members of St. Martin's did it up in needlepoint for me and I still have it framed.

The General Convention approved the book and, as is required by our church law, it was brought up for a second reading in 1979 and gained final approval. The 1979 Book of Common Prayer appropriated many of the fruits of the liturgical movement and incorporated the learnings from the season of experimentation that had preceded it. It is still referred to by some longtime church members as "the new prayer book."

My election as a deputy to the 1976 General Convention led to my involvement in the larger world of national church life as I came to know people from all around the country. I served on various commissions, including one that dealt with liturgy and another with ecumenical relations. In 1984 I was asked to allow my name to be forwarded to the committee responsible for nominating those who would be on a slate for the election of the next bishop of the Diocese of Chicago. The bishop elected would serve with the then current bishop,

James Winchester Montgomery, and then succeed Bishop Montgomery when he retired.

It is quite usual for clergy to protest that the episcopal office is the last thing they ever want. "Me, a bishop?" I would venture to say this posture covers up some secret hopes to the contrary. However, for whatever reason, I had never seriously entertained the idea of becoming a bishop. Perhaps this was because my sense of vocation, and indeed my sense of self, were deeply rooted in being a parish priest whose care and concern was focused upon those I had been called to serve and to guide as they explored in personal and corporate ways what it meant to be followers of Jesus. Now, I had to face the possibility, however unlikely, that I might be elected a bishop.

When the election process started, potential nominees were sent a series of questions. It seemed to me that answering the questions would indicate my active interest in becoming a bishop. Further, if I opened myself to the possibility and was not elected, I would then have to return to my congregation perceived as one who had been ready to abandon them for the sake of "advancement." With all this roiling about I went to see my spiritual director, Gary Brophy. I told him why I thought I should not answer the questions. He listened to me patiently and then said, "Frank, you're a coward." He told me that unless I knew some fundamental reason why it would be wrong to allow myself to be considered, I should answer the questions, put myself in a stance of availability, and let the community make its decision. He said I would have to deal with the poverty of being chosen or the poverty of not being chosen, and that, either way, it would be an experience of spiritual poverty. He was exactly right. If I was not elected I would have to deal with the fact that the community did not see within me the appropriate giftedness and ability. If I was elected, I would most likely be stretched well beyond what I perceived to be my capacities and gifts.

As it turned out, I was nominated, and then elected. The election took place on a Saturday. That afternoon I got a phone call from Chicago with the news. That evening I played the role of Snoopy the dog in a parish production of *You're a Good Man,*

Charlie Brown. This was well before the days of the Internet and the congregation did not yet know what had happened that afternoon. I planned to tell them the next morning. So that evening I sat on my doghouse and said: "Yesterday I was a dog. Today I am a dog. Tomorrow I'll probably still be a dog. There's so little hope of advancement." Even as I spoke the lines in my dog voice, the irony of the moment was full upon me.

Chicago Years

For you I am a bishop, but with you I am a Christian.
One is a danger, the other is salvation.
—St. Augustine of Hippo

The day after I was elected I was in a state of turmoil. Somewhat in the spirit of Mary, who after the angel Gabriel told her she had been chosen to give birth to the Son of God rushed off to see her kinswoman, Elizabeth, I knew I needed to share what had happened with someone I could trust. So I went to see the Quaker philosopher Douglas Steere. I had met him several years earlier when we were both speakers at a conference on prayer, and I greatly admired his deep and wise spirit. I particularly felt the need to talk to someone not involved in the life of the Episcopal Church who could help me look with detachment at what had happened and find my grounding. I knew he would not be invested on my behalf in what might appear to be the next step in a ladder upward, and that a hierarchical ministry held little fascination for him. Our conversation focused on the spiritual aspects of what lay ahead, and his insights and encouragement proved invaluable. He was one of the many along the way from religious traditions different from my own who have been word-bearers to me.

At this time of transition, I sought out another trusted word-bearer and went to Mount Saviour to see Father Martin Boler. I particularly sought out Father Martin because I knew he was familiar with the ministry of care and oversight, albeit of a religious community rather than a diocese. I was not disappointed in my visit. Our conversation was foundational to

me as I began my episcopal ministry. I wrote down his words
of counsel and have gone back to them again and again over
the years.

> Frank, be yourself. Others will show you your
> weaknesses. Do not become perfectionistic. God
> reveals his glory through your weaknesses. Don't
> become dejected by your failures. If God wants you
> to be a bishop, then God will be with you in spite
> of everything. You are called to be real. Trust in
> God, not in your own ability, though you must not
> be passive.

Grateful for his wisdom, I set off for my new life as a bishop in
Chicago, a city I had visited briefly as a teenager. My episcopal
ordination occurred on March 2, 1985, the Feast of St. Chad,
who had been the bishop of Litchfield, England, in the seventh
century. St. Chad was known for his humility, which he expressed
by refusing the local king's directive that he travel on horseback
to visit his congregations. He preferred to walk, meeting people
on their own level in an unhurried way. I thought to myself: what
an excellent model for a new bishop, particularly in a world where
efficiency has largely overruled notions of leisurely attention.

It was the custom at ordinations in the Diocese of Chicago for
prayer cards to be given to the congregation as a reminder of the
occasion, and as an invitation to pray for the person ordained.
To that end, I designed a card that drew together an image and
a text. The image was of a mother pelican piercing her breast to
feed her young with her blood. This image symbolized Christ's
self-gift of his body and blood in the Eucharist and was popular
in the Middle Ages, based on the ancient legend that mother
pelicans did indeed feed their young with their own blood.
The image was familiar, as it had been embroidered on one of
the hangings in the chapel at St. Paul's School. I also chose it
because it is maternal; though a bishop may be male, he must

also be able to exercise the sort of nurturing and tenderness our culture associates with motherhood.

The text accompanying the image was drawn from the writings of the great Brazilian Roman Catholic Archbishop, Dom Hélder Câmara. His words described the kind of bishop I intended to be:

> The bishop belongs to all. Let no one be scandalized
> if I frequent those who are considered unworthy or
> sinful. Who is not a sinner? Let no one be alarmed
> if I am seen with compromised and dangerous
> people on the left or the right. Let no one bind
> me to a group. My door, my heart must be open to
> everyone. Absolutely everyone.

Little did I realize when I chose these words the cost involved in living them. And so, naive, I started into episcopal ministry in a diocese filled with contradictions and paradoxes and multiple points of view. It opened me to a world of one hundred forty-one congregations stretching across the upper third of the state of Illinois. All of the dynamics were there: urban, suburban, and rural, from affluence to poverty, embracing a wide diversity of backgrounds, races, ethnicities, gay and straight, liberal and conservative, all sorts and conditions of humanity representing a stunning array of theological perspectives and sensibilities. During the course of one Sunday I found myself in the morning sitting on a throne flanked by green silk curtains with a kneeling acolyte extending a silver salver in which I was to wash my hands; that afternoon I celebrated essentially the same liturgy sitting on a rusty folding chair in a high school gymnasium with a congregation that had yet to find a building of its own.

As I made my way through this jumble, I had to face and acknowledge my own biases and prejudices. I came to understand that I had different levels of ease and comfort in the situations and settings that were part of my new life. I was obliged to realize, with a growing sense of my own limitations, that my heart was simply not that open. I had to acknowledge that though I used the language of accessibility and welcome in many ways I could be judgmental and guarded. Reflecting now on all this I realize that God had led me to Dom Hélder's text for a purpose. What I thought of as something I could accomplish was, in fact, God's agenda with me yet to be lived out in what lay ahead.

Though Bishop Montgomery and I were shaped for ministry in somewhat different contexts, we were both grounded in the Catholic expression of Anglicanism. Because he was patient and welcoming to the new bishop he made my entry a time of grace. The fact that I had limited authority and was not "the bishop" gave me ease as I settled in to what would be a thirteen-year relationship with the clergy and people of the diocese. My years in Chicago stretched and fed me in many ways and taught me something of Christ's ability to reveal Christ's self in amazingly diverse and often challenging and paradoxical circumstances.

The Rev. Paul Wessinger of the Society of Saint John the Evangelist preached the sermon at my episcopal ordination. He had served as Superior of his community, and he, like Father Martin, was no stranger to the complexities of a ministry of care and oversight. With great feeling, he spoke about the impending loneliness I would experience as a bishop. I took his words to heart both as a reality I was approaching and as an invitation to guard against isolation.

Because my ordination took place during the school year, Phoebe and Eliza, age twelve, returned to Philadelphia, and Hannah, age seventeen, went back to St. Paul's School where she was a student. Without familial support, my first four months as bishop were indeed lonely. Another bishop had cautioned me that during your first months, given the strain of a new form of ministry, you are likely to gain weight and get sick. After a couple of months I found I could hardly button my new cassock. When the school year ended we regrouped as a family. I was so relieved with Phoebe's arrival in Chicago that what had been pent up during the previous months was unleashed and I promptly went to bed with a fever of 102 degrees. As I was recovering, I remember waking up in the night and being overwhelmed by all that lay before me. Feeling sorry for myself,

I began to moan in hopes that Phoebe might wake up and offer me solace. Finally she opened one eye and asked if anything was wrong. I said, "I think being a bishop is going to kill me." Phoebe replied, "Isn't that what it is all about?"—and promptly went back to sleep. I thought to myself that she was right. It is all about dying and rising with Christ. I felt a wave of peace and went back to sleep myself. Here again was an instance of how the Spirit can address us directly through those who are most intimately part of our lives.

This was a time of huge transition for the four of us as we felt ourselves uprooted from all that was familiar. Though my role as bishop was well defined, there were no expectations, and no role, for the wife of the bishop, as Bishop Montgomery was unmarried. Phoebe had to create new patterns for herself. One of our joint efforts was a conference for clergy and spouses, which allowed participants to know us more informally as "Frank and Phoebe," rather than "the bishop and his lovely wife."

Though Phoebe was often unable to visit different congregations with me on Sundays because Eliza was still at home, she became involved in the life of the Cathedral and the diocese. One of her concerns was to raise awareness about the high number of violent deaths of children in the city. Early during our time in Chicago, she was hired to direct the Chicago office of Heifer International, an organization dedicated to eliminating world hunger largely through supplying farm animals to needy communities around the world.

Meanwhile, rather than going to the Cathedral with Phoebe on Sundays, Eliza decided to join a new school friend of hers at one of the few churches in the diocese that regularly had Morning Prayer rather than Eucharist as its main Sunday service. I will never forget Eliza returning from her first experience of worship there and saying with some indignation: "What was that service? There was no bread and wine. And, what was that strange language?" It dawned on me then that my daughter had never been exposed to any service other than the Eucharist in its contemporary language form.

Michael Marshall, a bishop of the Church of England, once observed that as parish clergy we were the stars but as bishops our role is to help others shine. Since no one can enter seminary declaring that they wish to be a bishop without being regarded with great suspicion, there is no advanced course offered on how to be a bishop. An early lesson for me was that being a bishop is not at all like being a parish priest on a larger scale, particularly in a diocese of the size and complexity of Chicago.

I soon came to understand the Office of Bishop was not mine personally but a *function* I shared with others, particularly the diocesan staff, who quickly became friends and trusted colleagues I relied on daily. It also became ever clearer as I moved from being a parish priest to being bishop of a large and complex diocese that I was not called to be everyone's personal pastor but rather a pastor of systems. My responsibility was to make sure that the various subsystems—such as finance, congregational development, care for clergy—were well ordered, accessible, and responsive.

I sought the expertise of an organizational consultant who, while sympathetic to the ministry and witness of the church, came at her work out of a Jewish background. She was not shy, therefore, in asking, "What exactly do you mean?" when some piece of ecclesiastical jargon was uncritically uttered. When in staff meetings we veered off into a nether land of abstraction, she would bring us back to earth with a recurring question: "What is the work?" This kept us grounded in the realities of what we were being called to attend to.

In addition to her competence, she had a playful spirit. Once at the end of a particularly intense consultation, she presented me with a gift. I opened the box and withdrew a pair of large, green furry dinosaur feet. "Just put them on," she said, "and then stamp your feet." I did so and the furry boots emitted loud growls and roars. "They're brute boots," she said, "and you will need them from time to time." She was right.

As Bishop of Chicago I was part of an ecumenical and

interfaith community of leaders whose ministries in many ways paralleled my own. As such they became friends and counselors. Among them was Rabbi Herman Shalman, who fled his native Germany to study in the United States as the fires of Nazism grew more intense. He was a man of great erudition and possessed an old-world graciousness. I remember during one of our lunches being overcome by a sense of blessing drawn from the depth and breadth of his spirit. I placed my hand on his and declared, "Herman, you are my Abba."

The then Roman Catholic Cardinal Archbishop of Chicago, Joseph Bernardin, also became a friend. His spirit was such that at the beginning of his ministry as Archbishop he stood before the congregation in the cathedral and declared simply, "I am Joseph, your brother." Though he honored the formal positions of the Roman Catholic Church, his pragmatic spirit could make allowances for the vagaries and complexities of the human condition. As a youth he had been educated in public rather than parochial schools. One of his high school classmates had become an Episcopal bishop and another a Lutheran bishop. Perhaps the secular education accounted for his generous ecumenical spirit. The first time he came for dinner with Phoebe and me, he asked if he could please take off his clerical collar and be comfortable. That willingness to be informal and "at home" characterized our relationship.

My first gathering with clergy was in one of the northern regions of the diocese. In preparation, I rather naively asked the priest planning the meeting what he wanted me to do. He said I should lead the group in a morning of reflection with meditation and silence and then, after lunch, share my vision for the diocese. I said I would be happy to oblige.

I had imagined a day with the clergy would be an "off-duty" day, so I arrived in jeans, not realizing that when the clergy met in the Diocese of Chicago they usually wore clerical attire. Here was the bishop in jeans, while the other clerics were more formally dressed, mostly in black suits and clerical collars. What they must have thought of their new bishop. As we began I realized how little I knew about the eighteen people sitting in a circle around the room so I suggested that we might start the day by sharing something of how we each had discerned a call to ordained ministry. My suggestion caught them by surprise. This was not at all what they had expected. To get things going, I decided to go first, giving the introverts time to organize their thoughts. I described something of my path to ordained ministry and then we started around the circle. Shortly after 1 p.m. one of the women preparing lunch looked in anxiously and inquired if we were ever going to eat. At that point we had only gotten about a quarter of the way around the circle. By the end of the day, nine of the eighteen had shared something of their story so we set a date for a second gathering. At the end of the afternoon several of the clergy told me how moved they were by these personal stories, and how glad they were to know one another at a deeper and more personal level. There is an enormous value to pastors in reconnecting with what first moved our hearts to discipleship with Christ.

This sharing is not only of value to pastors but to all of us who are seeking to be faithful in living more fully the deep mystery of who we are called to be. Listening to the stories of others, and teasing out our own story, is a holy act, reminding us of how we have been "nipped in the heel" by Christ who pursues us, as described by the English poet Francis Thompson in his classic 1893 poem, "The Hound of Heaven." In so doing, we bring once again to mind how the Spirit has implanted in us a desire, a fascination, a sense of longing, an awareness of being drawn beyond ourselves into a mysterious reality that can exceed both our expectations and our understanding.

This is an instance of reading the scripture of our own lives in the fellowship of others. In so doing, we can enrich and enlarge one another's recognition and appreciation of what God, often in subtle ways, has been up to in our lives. At the same time, an event in my own life and how I have lived it may become an illumination and a gift to someone else. Once again, we are reminded that our lives are linked together and that I can come to a better knowledge of myself not through isolated self-scrutiny but by opening my life to others.

———

One of the responsibilities of an Episcopal bishop is to visit all the congregations of the diocese. During my first year in Chicago before I made my Sunday visitation I would call ahead to ask about the liturgy at which I would preside. "It's just the usual thing," I would be told, only to find upon arrival that often "the usual" was, at least in my experience, wildly unusual. I soon came to realize that every congregation had its own character, temperament, and liturgical tradition. I could sense from such things as body language and level of participation if a congregation was passive or actively engaged. A particularly telling moment came when as the preacher I looked out at the congregation from the pulpit. If there was a spirit of eagerness and expectation, I knew the people were accustomed to lively and life-giving preaching. But, if I looked out and saw little shades going down over all their eyes, I knew they expected to receive very little.

Early on, I visited one of the latter sort of congregations in an affluent suburb. As I began my sermon I became aware of a great gulf between me and the congregation. Their shades were down. In a rather frenzied effort to break through I became ever more energetic and began to flail about vigorously in an effort to coax them into wakefulness. In the process, I inadvertently struck my hand against the side of the pulpit. At that point, the sound system, which was particularly fine-tuned and no doubt able to compensate for hearing deficiencies on the part of older members of the congregation, sent forth a resounding crack, evoking gasps. This made me further agitated. Without even thinking I stopped and held up my hand to show them the enormous amethyst bishop's ring that belonged to the Diocese of Chicago. I said, "You see this ring? No decent woman would wear a stone like this before five o'clock in the afternoon." I was echoing the quip made by a friend of mine, the master of ceremonies for the Roman Catholic Archbishop of Philadelphia, when he saw the ring. At this point, I was totally appalled with my performance.

And then I heard a small titter from the congregation, which turned into a full-throated roar of laughter. I joined in, and from then on the congregation was on the tiptoe of expectation. Again and again, often at awkward moments, I have been made aware that laughter has the power to open us to one another and draw us together, even in the midst of a very formal liturgy.

During one Sunday visit I sat in the bishop's chair behind the altar and spooned incense into the brass thurible held by a teenage acolyte who stood in front of me with his back to the congregation. An unholy gleam played across his youthful face as out of his mouth came an enormous bubble of pink bubble gum. It was so large that it hid his whole face. Then, with a loud sucking sound, he drew it all back into his mouth. Fortunately, the singing of the choir covered the gum popping. He fixed me with an expression filled with wicked playfulness. *This is outrageous*, I thought to myself. Then, it occurred to me that perhaps this untoward event was really about Jesus inviting me to relinquish my judgmental spirit. If Jesus, as we are told in the gospels, could use mud and saliva to restore the sight of the blind, why could he not use bubble gum to liberate me from my liturgical rectitude? This experience was extremely liberating and allowed me to go hither and yon with a new spirit. When I smiled, I smiled genuinely. If bizarre and wild things happened, I realized it was how the congregation played. Indeed, liturgical worship is a form of sacred play. After all, in the Book of Proverbs, Wisdom is described as playing continually before the throne of God. Entering into the sacred play of the local congregation gave me the freedom to meet Christ in ways I had previously been unable to acknowledge because of my rigidity and preconceptions about how things ought to be.

———

Since it is by God's mercy that we are engaged in this ministry, we do not lose heart.

—2 Corinthians 4:1

Even though I had read these words of Paul many times, they came home to me with the force of a personal address at a moment when I most needed to hear them. On a cold autumn weekday I drove an hour and a half west from Chicago in the late afternoon to preside at a confirmation service. The traffic was heavy, the rain intense, and I had a bad cold. In short, I felt sorry for myself and resentful that I had said "yes" to this mid-week liturgy. After fortifying myself with a greasy hamburger and some limp French fries, I headed to the church and discovered that the readings chosen for the liturgy were not the ones I expected. Seized with irritation I went off to the priest's study to read the lessons he had chosen in preparation for what would now be a completely extemporaneous homily. One of the readings included those words now so important to me: "Since it is by God's mercy that we are engaged in this ministry, we do not lose heart."

The passage continues: "We have this treasure in clay jars so that it may be made clear that this extraordinary power belongs to God and does not come from us." Paul's words touched on the vulnerability I felt at that moment and spoke directly to my feelings. He also speaks about being afflicted but not crushed. This flushed out from hiding my feelings of resentment and self-pity. Through it all, my overwhelming sense was of God's mercy, which had called and sustained me and brought me to this very moment. Greasy hamburger and limp French fries aside, it was a moment of grace and insight. Here again, I saw the subtle workings of the Holy Ghost.

Sign and Symbol . . . Role and Person

It is true in many positions of leadership that the leader, like it or not, becomes sign and symbol and thus must remain clear about the distinction between person and role. I experienced this during my years as a parish priest, and the need for clarity in this regard is even more urgent when one puts on episcopal regalia. Indeed the possibilities for self-adornment fill the pages of catalogues dedicated exclusively to what bishops might wear. I slowly learned that the more elaborate the wardrobe, the higher the miter, the more grand the title, the more stripped you become within yourself. And what a paradox this is. Bishops are given a symbolic role and elevated externally. However, "care for all the churches" and living that role can put bishops in touch with their spiritual poverty in unanticipated ways. God's grace is often revealed when we feel least competent within ourselves.

It is the custom in the Diocese of Chicago for portraits of the bishops to be hung at the Diocesan Center. Accordingly, my portrait was commissioned and then unveiled at a reception. As I stood looking at myself looking back at me from an ornate gold frame, a woman approached me, declared the portrait a great likeness and exclaimed, "It captures all of your joy!" A few minutes later, another woman stood beside me and, in tones of commiseration, told me that the portrait "radiates all of the suffering you have had to bear!" Hmm. I looked again at the portrait and wondered how either woman had been able to draw from it what she thought she saw. It seemed at that moment how people saw me in a picture frame was a metaphor for what I experienced in my person. I was the subject of people's projections. They saw what they expected to see. I was me, Frank, but for some I existed solely as the Bishop of Chicago. Role and person do coexist, of course, and there needs to be coherence and unity between them. However, I had to learn that people's attitudes and responses to me, particularly when they were upset or discontented, quite often had more to do with my symbolic role than with me as a person. This says to me how important it is for people who play symbolic roles to learn the distinction between themselves and the role they are called to play.

Over the years I have kept in mind what a Jesuit friend once said to me: "What other people say about you is none of your business." This has been a saving word, and an admonition to remain equally detached from extravagant praise and excoriating criticism. This does not mean that one should not be open to receiving difficult or challenging truth that may come in the form of a critique. However, one's sense of self should not rise and fall with each positive or negative comment.

As a bishop I became a member of the Episcopal Church's House of Bishops, which gathers twice a year. In listening to my fellow bishops I was struck by how beleaguered a number of them felt, and what a sense of community they derived from their connection with other bishops. Most of us had been called to the episcopate from the world of the parish and the fact that we had been "successful" parish priests had counted in our favor at the time of election. As parish clergy we had been accustomed to a continuing community in which to preach and preside at the liturgy. Our sense of worth was derived, in large measure, from the support, appreciation, and affection of the members of our congregations. If something went awry in the life of the congregation we could usually deal with it directly. But, as bishops we were removed from that ongoing familiarity and intimacy and support. For many bishops the highpoint of their ministry is the Sunday visit to one of their congregations because it is the closest they come to the life they knew as parish clergy.

My involvements beyond the diocese included serving on the planning committee for meetings of the House of Bishops. During one of our planning sessions, I made some observations that the then Presiding Bishop, Edmond Browning, asked me to share with the full body. My topic was "murmuring"—an allusion to the murmuring and complaining that the children of Israel indulged in during their forty years of wandering in the wilderness. They grieve for the loss of the security they had known in Egypt, even though they had been slaves. They complain to Moses and accuse him of leading them into the desert to die. He in turn rails against the heavens and blames God for having put him in this position. I noted that in unsettling times members of the congregation murmur and complain to their priest, who in turn murmurs and complains to the bishop, and the bishops then murmur and complain to the Presiding Bishop. I went on to say I had no idea what the Presiding Bishop does with all the murmuring, but perhaps he follows Moses's example. Perhaps he goes out onto the parapets of his residence on the top floor of 815 Second Avenue in New York and rails against the heavens. Little did I know that I was soon to find out what the Presiding Bishop did in response to murmuring.

A New Chapter

We may never see the end results, but that is the difference between the master builder and the worker. We are workers, not master builders: ministers, not messiahs. We are prophets of a future not our own.

—Archbishop Oscar Romero

Having experienced the "poverty of being chosen" in the Chicago election, I assumed I would never again have to go through anything as disruptive to my family and me. As it turned out, this was an erroneous assumption. When I was asked if I would allow my name to go forward as a nominee for the nine-year term as the Presiding Bishop I agreed, remembering the counsel of Gary Brophy about standing in a place of availability and allowing the community to make the decision. Subsequently, I was nominated, and went through three unsettling months leading up to the election, which occurred in the midst of the General Convention in July 1997.

The Presiding Bishop is elected by the bishops following a celebration of the Eucharist. On this occasion the House of Bishops gathered in historic Christ Church, Philadelphia. Interestingly, William White, an early rector of Christ Church, became the first Presiding Bishop in 1789, and his remains lie buried before the altar. In a wonderful bit of irony, this was the very church where years before I had overseen several diocesan liturgies.

We five nominees were driven in a van to Christ Church, and we found our places among the bishops who were milling about in conversation. As I stood in the center aisle I noticed Steven Plummer, a Navajo bishop, sitting quietly in one of the pews. I thought I would sit by him and allow his peaceful spirit to shield me. A few minutes later another figure appeared. Creighton Robertson, the Bishop of South Dakota, and a Sioux, entered our pew and sat on the other side of me. These two Native American bishops, unaffected by the spirit of urgency around us, exuded a quiet presence that was a tremendous gift to me. After the third ballot the results were announced. I had been elected and the bishops stood and applauded. Creighton then leaned over and whispered in my ear: "It would be appropriate for you to stand now."

———————

Before the election I had accepted an invitation from Sophia Cavalletti, an Italian scripture scholar and one of the founders of the Catechesis of the Good Shepherd, to serve as a chaplain at their upcoming conference in Italy. The Catechesis is an international program of spiritual formation for children based on principles developed by Maria Montessori. The conference was to take place not long after the election and I looked forward to it, thinking it would either be a consolation if I was not elected, or a welcome respite before the beginning of a new chapter. The fact that the gathering was to be held in Assisi, the city of Saints Francis and Clare, made the invitation even more attractive.

"Let Assisi be your atrium," Sophia advised us upon our arrival. "Atrium," in the parlance of the Catechesis, is the classroom, or more accurately the environment, the space, which serves to foster and support encounters with the mystery of God. "Let Assisi be your atrium," I said quietly to myself that first evening as I set out from my hotel for a walk. Within a few minutes I found myself standing before the entrance of the Church of Santa Chiara. Entering the church, I saw a sign over a doorway in the south wall: *The crucifix that spoke to St. Francis.*

Moved more by curiosity than devotion, I entered the darkened chapel and there, illuminated by a single spotlight, was the painted crucifix from the Church of San Damiano where Francis had prayed at the beginning of his conversion. I was drawn to the figure on the cross as if it were a magnet. I moved from observer to participant, and from a pew to a *prie-dieu* at the foot of the cross. After some moments I looked down and saw that a prayer, in four languages, had been affixed to its top. It was a prayer written by Francis himself before this very cross:

> Most high, glorious God, enlighten the darkness of my heart and give me true faith, certain hope, and perfect charity, sense and knowledge, so that I may carry out your true and holy will. Amen.

In the silence of the chapel, the prayer became my own, and a preparation for what might lie ahead.

Each morning I got up early and made my way to the cross. I had to be there and pray Francis's prayer. Partway through the week I wondered, "What did the crucifix say to Francis?" One afternoon I wandered by chance into a small square and noticed a plaque on a nearby wall. Here was my answer. Christ had said, "Francesco, *va ripara la mia chiesa* . . . Francis, go repair my Church." I was overcome and in tears, tears of recognition that this was the call, the invitation, the strange attraction of a twelfth-century crucifix. At the same time I was skeptical. Did an overwrought Frank Griswold, who had had too much Assisi, create a moment of high drama and emotion, or did this come from the Spirit?

Later that evening I shared what had happened with a Roman Catholic nun at the conference. I got no further than saying, "I was praying in front of the San Damiano crucifix . . ." when she declared with unquestioning certainty, "That's it; that's your vocation. Repair the church." Here was the confirming human word I needed before I could allow Christ's words to Francis to find a home in me.

Me? Repair the church? What might this mean? Such arrogance, what an unbearable burden, what an impossibility, what an invitation to fantastical projections and unrealizable expectations. I wanted to confine Christ's daunting command to the life of St. Francis where it properly belonged. But I have learned over the years that moments of resistance and unsettlement are almost always invitations to deeper prayer and greater availability to the motions of the Spirit. And so I gave the words to Francis the freedom to be addressed to me: "Frank, go repair my church." As I did so I was made profoundly aware that the task belongs to all who seek to follow Jesus.

What does it mean to repair the church, to do the continuing work of rebuilding? There are, of course, many possible answers. What was to become ever clearer to me over my nine-year term as Presiding Bishop is that the church is not an object or an institution to be fixed or a building to be repaired, as Francis himself first thought. Instead the church is a relationship to be lived: it is a relationship of communion established by God through Christ in the power of the Holy Spirit which finds expression and is made incarnate—is earthed and given flesh—in our communion, our fellowship, with one another. As such, the church is always, in every age, being rebuilt and reformed out of the struggles and witness and imperfect fidelity of its members. "Repair" meant for me the work of strengthening and deepening the unalterable bond established between us because of our common baptism and despite our differences. "Repair" meant living a life of communion that both transcends and includes different theological positions and ways of embodying and living the gospel. It meant a costly living of Paul's metaphor of the church as the body of Christ of which we are all essential limbs and members.

My investiture as Presiding Bishop occurred on January 10, 1998, at the Cathedral Church of St. Peter and St. Paul in Washington, D.C., also known as the National Cathedral. As that solemn occasion faded into the background, I became more and more aware of the many responsibilities and expectations that went with the office I had assumed. I found myself returning often to the words Christ had addressed to Francis about repairing the church, and reflecting on how I was to do my part to honor that call.

—————

I slept and dreamt that life was joy.
I awoke and saw that life was service.
I acted and behold,
Service was joy.

—Rabindranath Tagore

The title, Presiding Bishop, hardly begins to describe what the office embraces. It includes serving as the chief pastor of the Episcopal Church and as its Primate, which is the title given to the chief bishop of each of the 39 provinces of the Anglican Communion around the world in 165 countries. Unsurprisingly, humorous references are frequently made to other creatures known as primates.

As Primate it was my responsibility to represent the Episcopal Church in other parts of the Anglican Communion. Because my visits were designed such that I might share in the daily life and ministry of the local churches, they were quite unlike tourist visits, and gave me a down-to-earth look at life in widely different and often challenging contexts. The visits also allowed me to bring what I learned and experienced back to inform the life and mission of the Episcopal Church, and to strengthen the bonds that hold us together globally.

In addition to fellow Anglicans, I frequently spent time with representatives of other faith communities and government leaders. I saw grassroots efforts to alleviate suffering, often carried out with great faith, unwavering commitment, and severely limited resources. For example, I was once invited to meet with representatives of the World Bank to discuss how the on-the-ground reality of Anglican dioceses around the world could be a more effective way of distributing aid than through local government agencies.

Along the way I discovered that the Presiding Bishop is the sign and symbol not only of the Episcopal Church but also of what are perceived as positive and negative dimensions of the United States and its global reach. I began to see aspects of this country and our role in the world through the eyes of others. Though I had been brought up to believe that we can only do good in the world, I began to see that some of our policies could harm other nations, and are not always locally perceived as beneficial.

Once I visited an African archbishop who had established, at his own expense, a compound surrounding his home to house and care for children who had lost their parents to HIV/AIDS. As he led me through the village, stopping along the way to show me where the children lived and ate, he turned to me and with great sadness, and some anger, asked: "Why has your nation sided with pharmaceutical companies against making anti-retroviral drugs, which we so desperately need, available at cost?" I had no answer.

Shortly after returning home from this visit, during a newspaper interview I said we were sometimes loathed in other parts of the world. In retrospect, the term I used was unduly harsh, but the remembrance of the village and the Archbishop's query were still burning in my consciousness. The interview, which included my remark, found its way into a White House press conference and subsequently led to a challenge to my point of view by one highly placed government official. He wrote me, taking exception to what I had said and informing me that everywhere he had traveled in the world he had been thanked for all the good we did. I responded and told him of my conversation with the African Archbishop.

Understandably, international visits by our president and other high government officials typically include only what their hosts wish them to see and to hear. In contrast, in my visits to brother and sister Anglicans in other parts of the world I have not been shielded from poverty, suffering, and the darker sides of the human condition. At the heart of such visits is the awareness that our relationship in Christ is grounded in St. Paul's vision of the church as a vast many-membered body in which suffering in any part is felt by the whole. Sadly, such a vision of our mutuality is not universally abroad in these times within our global community.

———————

Many people, both within and outside religious institutions, assume that those who head them are bureaucrats and thinly disguised secular CEOs, a view I somewhat shared until I became one myself. Any hint of that was dispelled when I was asked to join a number of other denominational heads at their annual two-day retreat. It was held at a place familiar to me: the College of Preachers on the grounds of the National Cathedral in Washington. I accepted the invitation to join the group with some reluctance, assuming the meeting would be filled with denominational statistics and a display of achievements and accomplishments.

By common consent, the first day of the meeting was spent in silence and prayer. When on the second day we came together to reflect on our day of retreat it became clear that all of us had an active prayer life. And none of us, though we took our ministries of leadership and oversight seriously, were so personally identified with our institutions that we had lost a sense of who we were as spiritual beings in need of constant communion with the Reality that transcended the institutions we oversaw. We were all engaged in some form of spiritual direction, in most cases from members of Roman Catholic religious communities. Candor and frankness are often more forthcoming with someone outside of your own religious tradition who sees you first and foremost in your personhood rather than in your role. My Jesuit spiritual directors over the years have dealt with me simply as Frank, a disciple of Jesus, and have little investment in my being an Episcopal bishop.

During our meetings conversation centered on the burdens of leadership and how easy it is to become consumed by the tensions within our denominations, particularly around issues of sexuality. We helped one another to see that the call to leadership and the demands placed upon us—not to mention the expectations of our constituencies—obliged us to face our own limitations and to seek that deeper grounding as persons of faith, without which our leadership could become "waterish, bleak and thin," in the words of George Herbert.

Our times together reminded me that, whatever our responsibilities, we could not shoulder them alone, and indeed we were not expected to. The words of the risen Christ to St. Paul are meant for us as well: "My grace is sufficient for you, for my power is made perfect in weakness." (2 Corinthians 12:9) However, accepting our weaknesses, our spiritual poverty, is not an invitation to some sort of passive resignation. There is no "poor me" in this. As Paul tells us: "For whenever I am weak, then I am strong." We are meant to be actively engaged, in the midst of what Paul names as "insults, hardships, persecutions and calamities for the sake of Christ." Our strength does not come solely from our own psychological, intellectual, or physical efforts, though they may well be called into play, but from the strength of the Spirit at work in us. At such times we may find that, in the words of Paul, we can do all things through Christ who strengthens us.

On September 10, 2001, Phoebe and I returned from a visit to my brother, Stephen, who lives in Italy. He had urged us to stay longer but September was going to be a busy month and so we headed home to New York. As it turned out, that was a fortuitous decision. The next morning, as was my custom, I attended Morning Prayer in the chapel of the Episcopal Church Center on Second Avenue in New York. Partway through the service a member of the staff came into the chapel and whispered to a colleague. I was both surprised and irritated, wondering why whatever he had to say couldn't wait. When the service ended I found out. A group of staff members were transfixed in front of a large television set in one of our conference rooms, looking at footage of the first tower of the World Trade Center ablaze. Then, a few minutes later, a second plane plowed into the other tower and what we had surmised at first to be a terrible accident we now knew was a deliberate attack. I can still feel the many emotions of that moment. Before the day was over I wrote a letter to the church. I include it here because—even after the passage of time—my sense of how we are called to be in the midst of a world where violence and hate are so easily unleashed remains unchanged:

> The events of this morning in New York City and Washington, D.C. make me keenly aware that violence knows no boundaries and that security is an illusion. To witness the collapse of the World Trade Center was to confront not only our vulnerability as a nation in spite of our power, but also the personal vulnerability of each of us to events and circumstances that overtake us. My heart goes out

to those who have been killed or injured, and to their stunned and grieving families and friends.

Our President has vowed to hunt down and punish those who are responsible for these depraved and wicked acts. Many are speaking of revenge. Never has it been clearer to me than in this moment that people of faith, in virtue of the Gospel and the mission of the Church, are called to be about peace and the transformation of the human heart, beginning with our own. I am not immune to emotions of rage and revenge, but I know that acting on them only perpetuates the very violence I pray will be dissipated and overcome.

Last week I was in Dublin where I found myself convicted by the photograph of a young girl in Northern Ireland being taken to school amid taunts and expressions of hatred because she was Roman Catholic. I know the situation in Northern Ireland is complex, and that religion is a convenient way of ordering hatred and justifying violence, but the tears running down the little girl's terrified face spoke to me of all the violence we commit in word and deed against one another—sometimes in the name of our God whose passionate desire is for the well-being and flourishing of all.

Expressions of concern and prayer have poured into my office from many parts of the world, in some instances from people who themselves are deeply wounded by continuing violence and bloodshed. I pray that the events of today will invite us to see ourselves as a great nation not in terms of our power and wealth but measured by our ability to be in solidarity with others where violence has made its home and become a way of life.

Yes, those responsible must be found and punished for their evil and disregard for human life, but through the heart of this violence we are called to another way. May our response be to engage with all our hearts and minds and strength in God's project of transforming the world into a garden, a place of peace where swords can become plowshares and spears are changed into pruning hooks.

Three days later, on September 14, a gray and rainy morning, Phoebe and I were driven in a pickup truck with a police escort from the Church Center down to what became known as Ground Zero. Our mission was to transport supplies from the Seamen's Church Institute, one of our Episcopal Church agencies in lower Manhattan, to various sites where rescue workers, National Guard members, police, and firefighters were dealing with the aftermath. As well, it was a symbolic "showing up," part of the work of those called to represent something larger than themselves.

The truck passed by St. Paul's Chapel of Trinity Church, St. Paul's being the oldest church building in Manhattan and the place where George Washington prayed after his inauguration. I noticed that the gate to the churchyard was ajar, and although there was debris and thick ash everywhere, I prevailed upon the driver to stop. I wanted to see if the church was open. We got out of the truck and went into the church. Nothing had been disturbed, not even a pane of glass broken even though the church is only a block from the World Trade Center. The graveyard behind the church had been devastated—trees uprooted, branches down, a thick layer of dust lay everywhere, covered by tiny pieces of paper. A fine dust had also settled over everything inside the building. I made my way to the sacristy, found a piece of paper, and wrote, "Just stopped by. Love and prayers, Frank Griswold, Presiding Bishop."

As I was leaving the priest in charge of the chapel appeared. We fell into one another's arms and he said, "I'm here. I'm just here, and the church is open." I replied, "Bless you. That's all you can do."

I looked over his shoulder and my eyes fell upon the brass crucifix above the altar. Suddenly I had the sense that Jesus's small brass arms could contain the hatred, violence, and anger, as well as the anguish and grief: all of the causes and consequences of that horrific event. It wasn't up to us to bear it alone because One had already borne it before us.

September 14 is the Feast of the Holy Cross, and earlier that morning I had celebrated the Eucharist in the chapel of the Seamen's Church Institute. In the gospel reading appointed for the day Jesus cries out, "And I, when I am lifted up from the earth, will draw all people to myself." (John 12:32) The outstretched arms of the crucifix and Jesus's words came together for me in the stillness of the chapel. In that moment I felt certain that only God could contain all this horror. In Christ God was reconciling the world to himself, as Paul tells us. We are called to live that mystery of reconciliation in all its fullness and in so doing to participate in Christ's work of drawing all things to himself. We are active agents in removing the barriers that block and occlude what God has done in Christ. Here I picture a spring of water blocked by debris. Our role is not to create the spring but to remove the leaves and branches that prevent the water from flowing free.

During late October 2001, while our nation was still reeling from the catastrophic events of September 11, I flew to Jacksonville, Florida, to attend a meeting. I was grateful for the southern sun and warmth, and early one morning set out from my hotel room for a walk along a deserted beach. In my hand I held my Russian Orthodox prayer rope: a knotted cord made of black wool. I walked along, praying in a meditative way, repeating over and over the Jesus prayer: "Lord Jesus Christ, Son of God, have mercy on me a sinner." Suddenly I caught a glimpse of a man approaching the beach on a side path.

"He looks Middle Eastern," I thought, and felt a tremor of fear. As the thought went through my mind I felt guilty and ashamed. There I was—victim to the very paranoia that I, since the evil of 9/11, had been quick to condemn.

After a few minutes, I saw out of the corner of my eye that the man was slowly closing the distance between us. I kept my pace and soon he was by my side.

"Are you reading?" he asked.

Well, obviously I was not reading, but having seen the prayer rope he was asking what seemed a less intrusive question.

"No," I replied, "I'm praying."

There was a pause, then: "What are you praying?" he persisted.

"The Jesus Prayer."

"And what is that?" he asked.

"Lord Jesus Christ, Son of God, have mercy on me a sinner." I explained the prayer had originated in the Christian East.

"What happens when you pray?"

I thought for a moment before I replied. "I pray that my heart may be purified and that I may be made one with Christ."

We continued to walk as the waves rushed in and retreated, and he carefully considered what I had said. He then told me his father had used a string of beads similar to my cord as a stimulus to prayer.

"And what did your father pray?" I asked.

"He prayed, 'Allah, Allah, Allah' . . . "

"And what happened when he prayed?"

"He prayed that his heart might be purified and that he might be made one with Allah."

A deep joy welled up within me as I recognized the profound unity of our prayer, regardless of our different paths.

He then asked me what I was doing in Jacksonville and I told him I was there for a church meeting.

"Why are you at a church meeting?"

"Well," I explained, "I am the Presiding Bishop of the Episcopal Church."

"Presiding Bishop?" He looked quizzical.

"I guess you could say that I am the chief pastor of the Episcopal Church."

To my surprise my walking partner then told me that he too was a minister, and that after the attacks of 9/11 he had been invited to speak at the local Episcopal Church. He produced a business card and I learned that he was the Imam of the local Islamic Center. The card said "Hafiz," which means that he had memorized the Quran.

By now the sun was well up and it was time for me to turn back. As he walked away I felt the tremendous grace I had been given in the encounter. My anxiety had been transformed into friendship, and a sense of brotherhood. I knew our meeting had occurred because of prayer, which was a further grace. Had he not seen my prayer rope in hand he never would have approached me, and I would have been left the prisoner of my suspicions.

It was clear to me as I walked back to the hotel that prayer was an important weapon in dealing with the charged atmosphere in the aftermath of that fateful September day. So many emotions were at work within us: sadness, anger, grief, revenge, fear, and the sense that we were unsafe. The illusion of invulnerability had been brutally taken from us. To this day we are left searching for firm ground to stand upon. For me, prayer provides that ground because it roots us in the all-embracing mercy and compassion of God, which is at the center of all that is life-affirming and real.

The prayer I am talking about here is not the kind of partisan prayer that one side uses against another. Rather, it is the deep prayer the Holy Spirit prays in our hearts with "sighs too deep for words." This prayer comes from the core of our being and breaks us open to God's own longing for the "healing of the nations." Such prayer is dangerous because it gives freedom to the Spirit to search us out and to alter our perceptions, to take us beyond our fears into what the psalmist calls an "open space," and to catch us up into God's continuing and urgent work of *Tikkun Olam*—a Hebrew phrase meaning "repair of the world."

He who does not see things in their depth
should not call himself a radical.

—José Martí

In spite of the relationship, or lack of the same, that existed between our two countries, the Episcopal Church in the United States and the Iglesia Episcopal de Cuba have maintained a warm relationship. During my time as Presiding Bishop I visited Cuba and experienced firsthand the church's lively social mission and work, particularly in rural communities. One Sunday morning I preached at the Cathedral in Havana and told the congregation that the Episcopal Church formally opposed the U.S. embargo on humanitarian grounds. For many ordinary Cubans, an American voice that was focused on their welfare was unexpected and appreciated.

Portions of my sermon, which I preached in Spanish, were later aired on Cuban television. On the eve of Ash Wednesday I was at the home of the Bishop of Cuba. We had had dinner and I was preparing to take my leave as I was scheduled to preside at the liturgy early the next morning at the Cathedral. As we were sitting in the bishop's living room the phone rang. It was an aide of Fidel Castro who called to say that Castro wished to have a conversation with Bishop Griswold that evening and that we would be called around 10 p.m. to be given the details of time and place. At around 10:30 p.m. the phone rang again and I was asked to meet *El Commandante* at his office.

After formal introductions I said, "I'm delighted to see you again," which provoked a look of surprise on Castro's face. I explained that I had been standing on a bridge over the Charles River in Cambridge, Massachusetts, in 1959 with a cheering crowd, including many other Harvard students, who waved at him as he came up the river in a boat. In those days he was still regarded as a hero and the liberator of Cuba. He smiled and replied, "I always wanted a Ph.D. from Harvard!"

Our conversation was wide-ranging and largely philosophical rather than political, and included a discussion of the nature of truth. "Truth," he said, "is larger than any one person's perspective," an observation with which I completely agreed.

He referred with concern to a recent epidemic of avian flu and how it had a drastic effect upon the poor for whom poultry is a primary source of protein. He spoke positively of the people of the United States and their spirit, while taking strong exception to the policies of our government regarding Cuba.

He told me of the recent visit of Pope John Paul II and recounted the Pope's arrival amidst great ceremony. He said he was waiting on the tarmac at the airport and that as John Paul descended the stairs from his plane, Castro noticed the bottom step was rather high off the ground and feared the Pope might trip, particularly given his frailty. As the Pope reached the bottom step he stumbled and, breaking protocol, Castro said that he then rushed forward and caught the Pope in his arms. I wondered if there had been a photograph of that moment: something of a contemporary Pietà.

At the end of an intense two-and-a-half-hour conversation I said it was now Ash Wednesday and in just a few hours I was to preside and preach at the Cathedral, noting that we both needed to retire. He smiled and made the sign of the cross on his forehead and said, echoing the Ash Wednesday liturgy: "Ashes to ashes . . . Dust to dust . . . I was trained by the Jesuits."

As I prepared to leave he looked at me and exclaimed: "Who would have thought that either of us would have chosen the paths we have chosen." I responded: "Yes, who would have guessed that you would become a revolutionary and I a bishop?"

Unsurprisingly, in the way of institutions, the members of the Episcopal Church have not all welcomed change at the same pace. For some, change is experienced as loss of what is stable and familiar and provides a sense of security in an ever-changing world. For others, change is a sign of the ever-active presence of the Holy Spirit calling us into the future and opening the way to new discovery and growth. Various images of the church as being a repository of tradition or blazing a trail into the future have a great deal to do with our own temperaments. Some of us are predisposed to be cautious in the face of change while for others of us change cannot occur fast enough. In the midst of these different senses of what it means to be church I have been portrayed as both Satan and savior. I have been variously viewed as personally responsible for undermining the stability of the Episcopal Church, as a visionary leader pressing on into the future, and as too slow in embracing change.

As I became its Presiding Bishop, the incendiary issue in the Episcopal Church, and in other mainline churches, concerned those whose patterns of affection were ordered to members of the same sex and who did not choose celibacy. Could such gay and lesbian persons serve as icons and ministers of Christ's presence in the church and the world? Some took their stand based on a plain reading of certain passages of scripture while others looked to the fruit of the Spirit as made manifest in lives lived in committed relationships with partners of the same sex. Given the breadth of my travels and experiences with differences within the church and the larger Anglican Communion, I felt it was important to remind the church that what some saw as normative and beyond question could also be looked at from other perspectives and lead people of faith to very different conclusions.

I also felt it important to acknowledge that sexuality is not an "it." We are all sexual beings and it is not news to anyone that our sexuality can confront us with desires and emotions that transcend our intellect and can play havoc with our notions of our proper selves. Given this, each one of us is faced with the question: how am I being called to live out my sexuality? Whatever our experience of this dimension of our personality, it is woven into our attitudes and opinions about questions of sexuality.

When scripture describes Jesus as having been "tempted in every way as we are," I assume that he too, in the fullness of his incarnate life, was a sexual being and subject to the same passions as are we all. The question we might ask ourselves is how our sexuality, incorporated into the fullness of our lives, can manifest the values of the gospel and yield the genuine fruit of the Spirit.

As the debate on sexuality continued in the Episcopal Church—emitting various levels of heat and light—I tried to bring into conversation those of different, and often passionately held, theological views. My hope was that the various factions might recognize Christ's presence in one another and be reconciled in spirit, even in the midst of their disagreements. It became clear that parliamentary procedure and Robert's Rules of Order, by which so many ecclesiastical gatherings are governed, were woefully unsuited to the subtle process of seeking truth in love. For the conversation to proceed, all parties needed an environment, a safe container, where the various faithful factions had the space to discern that truth is often larger, and more complex, than any one point of view.

The annual five-day retreats of the bishops, which drew some 250 bishops to a remote rural setting, provided just such a container. Integral to our gatherings was the time and attention given to worship. The constant reminder that we were rooted and grounded together in Christ freed us from being imprisoned in the limitation of our own opinions. Morning and Evening Prayer marked the beginning and ending of each day, while at midday we gathered for a Eucharist. Conversations around small tables built a broad spirit of mutual respect. We worked together at opening our hearts to one another and listening to other points of view. My hope was that the fruit of these experiences would provide bishops with the perspective to guide their dioceses through a difficult season.

A pivotal moment in the life of the Episcopal Church occurred in the spring of 2003 when the people of the Diocese of New Hampshire elected V. Gene Robinson as their next bishop. He had served in New Hampshire for many years as an assistant to the bishop and was well known and respected. However, as he was a partnered gay man, the election brought national attention to the life of the Episcopal Church and its workings, and brought to a boil the simmering struggles over sexuality.

That summer bishops and the lay and clergy representatives from each of our 114 dioceses—an assembly of more than 1,000 people—gathered in Minneapolis for the General Convention.

For Gene Robinson to be ordained and consecrated as bishop of New Hampshire, it was necessary according to church law for a majority of the bishops and deputies to give their formal consent.

Given the strong feelings that the New Hampshire election had provoked, I decided that before asking the bishops to consider their consent we should spend several hours in a carefully ordered exercise of discernment. We would invite the Holy Spirit to give us, personally and collectively, the interior freedom to see both the negative and positive dimensions of the decision that lay before us. After an initial period of prayer I asked the bishops to reflect on the potential negative consequences of consenting to the ordination. Even those who were strongly in favor were able to perceive some of the potential negative effects, particularly in relation to other churches of the worldwide Anglican Communion where views on homosexuality were strongly negative. After the potential negative consequences were put forth without debate, we took a recess. Following another period of prayer for the guidance of the Spirit and, once again, interior freedom from one's personal biases, we examined the positive aspects of giving consent. We then looked together at both lists and discussed the weight and significance of the pros and cons. After which, again following a time of prayer, a majority of bishops gave consent to the ordination and consecration. When the result was announced I disallowed any expression of approval or disapproval.

When the bishops gathered the next day one stood and quietly said to us all: "Right now I am still in the Tomb. Please respect that and don't force me into the Resurrection." All who heard him respected his feelings, even if they did not share them.

This exercise in discernment, based largely on the wisdom of St. Ignatius Loyola, was conducted in a private session, without press or public. I like to believe the time spent in prayer and respectful conversation in which all voices and opinions were carefully expressed and honored helped to move us as a community of bishops into a new place beyond winning and losing. Sadly, some members of the church—including several active and retired bishops—felt that in light of the consent they could no longer remain within the fellowship of the Episcopal Church.

———

My nine-year term of office ended and in November 2006 I conveyed the primatial staff, the symbol of the office, to my successor, Katharine Jefferts Schori, the twenty-sixth Presiding Bishop and the first woman to serve as a primate in the Anglican Communion. As I did so I was aware of the immense privilege it had been to serve the church as its chief pastor. During those years my experience of the body of Christ had been greatly expanded and I had been deeply blessed by having encountered Christ in the limbs and members of his risen body in many places. I have been strengthened in my faith by their courage and witness, often in the midst of difficult circumstances and immense challenges. Thus began a new chapter in my life.

———

Over the years, I have been awarded honorary degrees by seminaries and universities at home and abroad, not to mention a variety of certificates and commendations acknowledging some honor or accomplishment. The one that means the most to me bears the image of Jesus the Good Shepherd and reads:

Frank Tracy Griswold
A Child of God, Marked as Christ's Own Forever
January 1, 1938.

In the broad sweep of my life and ministry, punctuated by small and large deaths and resurrections, calls to relinquishment which often became doorways to new discovery, this certificate reminds me again and again of my fundamental identity— of who, and in whom, I most truly am—Frank, child of God, marked as Christ's own forever.

Encountering the Divine

Wherever there is the taste for truth, there is God.
—St. Augustine of Hippo

To know that what is impenetrable to us really exists, manifesting itself as the highest wisdom and the most radiant beauty, which our dull faculties can comprehend only in their primitive forms—this knowledge, this feeling, is at the center of true religion.
—Albert Einstein,
The Merging of Spirit and Science

These days we hear someone declare that he or she is "spiritual but not religious" so often that the phrase has become something of a cliché. The notion of spirituality as separate and distinct from religion has developed great currency, which is understandable as it is the honest stance of so many thoughtful people. According to the Pew Research Center, the number of people who are unaffiliated with any religious body is continuing to grow at a rapid pace, with the number somewhere around one-fifth of the U.S. public and one-third of adults under thirty. At the same time, polling shows that of this unaffiliated group, two-thirds say they believe in God. What can this mean?

It seems to me that behind this separation of spirituality and religion is the intuition on the part of many, often called "seekers," that there is something transcendent and real beyond this world, something far more expansive and mysterious than what they experience as "religion," loosely defined, and most certainly not apparent to them in "organized religion."

In the Gospels there are accounts of those who come to the apostles and say, "we would see Jesus." For many individuals these days, Jesus is *not* someone they want to seek—at least not as they have been led to understand him. Jesus can present problems because of the way various groups have claimed the authority to speak about Jesus, and worse, to speak *for* Jesus, often in very condemning and judging terms. The use of religious language—often in theologically unsound ways—to bolster particular political positions makes it difficult for the multiple, contradictory voices of organized religion to be heard by those who are hungry for some authentic experience of the Divine. Nevertheless, some continue to seek, pressed on by some interior longing, a yearning toward something, for something, which might be described as an authentic experience of the transcendent.

Religious But Not Spiritual?

I must confess that I am continually surprised at how disconnected the life of the church can be from any living relationship with God. This brings up the deeper question of what it means to be "religious." We sometimes describe people as "religious" simply because they are caught up in a variety of external practices associated with religion. They go to church. They send their children to Sunday school. They support the local congregation financially. However, none of this may lay claim to their deeper patterns of behavior, or their response to the world around them. None of this may have anything to do with a living relationship with the mysterious force, the deep mystery of the universe known since time immemorial by many names. For me, the name is God. Believing this force exists is a first step. However, believing in God the way one might believe in the existence of the maple tree on the corner is not a commitment to a relationship. You can pass by the tree every day and take it for granted as a familiar object, to be either noticed or ignored.

In the Christian tradition the primary work of the Holy Spirit is to establish relationship, or communion, between us and this deep mystery. In the Gospel of John, Jesus declares himself to be the truth and not simply a teacher of truth. We encounter Jesus as truth through a process of mutual abiding: "he in us and we in him." What this calls for is a continuing and developing relationship, not a static declaration of belief.

It is not unusual for people, including those who would call themselves "religious," to construct the world in such a way that there is a separate "religious realm" that is stamped all over with the name of God. Next to it they see the realm of "ordinary life," made up of a sequence of what appear to be the singularly mundane events that are the stuff of our days. The disconnect here is that everything is potentially extraordinary and revelatory. Everything can be charged with what the Jesuit poet Gerard Manley Hopkins has described as "the grandeur of God," even the seemingly unexceptional and ordinary. Everything has the potential to be a sign or a symbol pointing beyond itself: inviting, disclosing, and engaging us. If Jesus could use water, word, human touch, bread, wine, a meal, and, yes, even mud and saliva, as means of encounter and revelation, then nothing in our world is off limits when it comes to ways in which God might seek to entice us and draw us into the force field of God's own loving and caring. Even what seems far removed from what we would ever consider the realm of the sacred can speak to us and reveal dimensions of God's presence.

Our self-confident and domesticated forms of religion can seem disconnected from the winds of the Spirit and the wildness of the Divine imagination. It is not by accident that Christ is referred to in the Book of Revelation as "the Lion of the tribe of Judah" (Revelation 5:5), nor is it hyperbole when the Letter to the Hebrews speaks of God as a "consuming fire" (Hebrews 12:29). No wonder many seekers, sensing that there is "more," are drawn to the meditative practices of eastern religions, which seem to respond to some of the deeper yearnings of the human spirit that too often go unacknowledged in the more active western tradition.

At the same time, here is a caution: a spirituality that is focused completely on one's own spiritual life and development can become a form of sanctified narcissism. A relationship with God has social consequences. Impelled by love, we look at the world through the eyes of God loving the world. Love gives itself away, so we must ask ourselves: in what active form am I called to articulate this love in my relationships with the world and people around me? In doing this we are not only serving God's larger purposes, we are growing more fully into who God is calling us to be. The Virgin Mary wasn't simply a convenient womb used for a divine purpose. Rather, through her *Yes* to becoming the mother of Jesus, she became more fully the very person she was called to be.

So it is with us—and with Jesus. Since, as scripture tells us, he was "in every respect" (Hebrews 2:17) like one of us with regard to his humanity, he had to discover, step-by-step, who he was through the events and encounters that overtook him. At the beginning of his ministry he saw himself sent to the lost sheep of the house of Israel. Then, he found himself confronted by a Gentile woman who asked him to cure her daughter. His response was: "It is not fair to take the children's food and throw it to the dogs," the children here being the children of Israel. She stood her ground and replied: "Even the dogs under the table eat the children's crumbs." Instead of being put out at her audacity, Jesus is convicted by her words and his vision is expanded as he comes to understand he has been sent to the Gentiles as well as to the Jews. With his enlarged consciousness provoked by this encounter, he tells her that her daughter has been healed (Matthew 15:21–28).

In classical spirituality, and indeed the scriptures, God's love, experienced and shared, is the fundamental invitation at the heart of authentic discipleship. Contemplation and action are wedded to one another and neither can be explicated without reference to its companion. Put another way, Mary and Martha, the biblical icons of contemplation and action, are sisters who together welcome Jesus into their home. It seems to me that in the present day much of western Christianity favors Martha over Mary: action over contemplation. Consequently, many who understand themselves as spiritual but not religious do not find their deepest longings satisfied by what the churches seem to offer. A broad range of secular groups heroically engage in good works of all kinds, including feeding the hungry, sheltering the poor, and protecting the environment. These concerns are in no way the special province of religion. However, when one is motivated out of communion and union with the Divine, this relationship sustains, deepens, and broadens our consciousness until we see as God sees, and act out of the power of God's love at work within us.

On the whole, I do not find Christians, outside of the catacombs, sufficiently sensible of conditions. Does anyone have the foggiest idea what sort of power we so blithely invoke? Or, as I suspect, does no one believe a word of it? The churches are children playing on the floor with their chemistry sets, mixing up a batch of TNT to kill a Sunday morning. It is madness to wear ladies' straw hats and velvet hats to church; we should all be wearing crash helmets. Ushers should issue life preservers and signal flares; they should lash us to our pews. For the sleeping god may wake someday and take offense, or the waking god may draw us out to where we can never return.
    —Annie Dillard, *Teaching a Stone to Talk*

My "profession" was, and still is, religion, which means I am one of those some call "professionally religious." I use this term myself from time to time, but with a touch of irony in it. This is because of my own history and, as I recounted earlier, the fact that what first drew me in this direction was not a religious institution, but a sense of the numinous, of something beyond the world I knew. I can only describe this "something" as mysterious and "other." What first drew me was my experience as a little boy being taken out for a walk, pushing open the red door of the church and standing, fascinated in that darkened space, awed by the feelings it engendered in me.

That same sense of being drawn by something beyond myself overtook me again at St. Paul's School. The solemnity of the liturgy, the thundering of the organ, the majesty and soaring height of the chapel; all spoke of mystery and transcendence. *In God's Presence*, the little book of prayers and practices given to me when I was confirmed, provided a way of responding to that sense of fascination as I was being allured by a force beyond myself, a force I was becoming able to name, with increasing confidence, as God.

The focal point of *In God's Presence* was the Eucharist, presented as a personal encounter with Christ in the seemingly innocent forms of bread and wine. Here I discovered the intersection of my life and the deep mystery that lay behind it which had fascinated and drawn me since childhood. Christ became the meeting point between my yearning toward mystery and the mystery itself.

I came to know the church not primarily as an institution, but as a community of worship, open and available to the Divine. I saw the church in its sacramental rather than its organizational reality. I saw that Jesus is ever present as the risen Christ in the sacramental actions of the church of which he is the head. The human institution of the church at its best is always pointing beyond itself to the spiritual reality—namely the risen body of Christ of which we are limbs and members by baptism. I saw the institution as the carrier of the mystery of God in Christ loving the world, and loving me as part of it. This has been the focus of my life ever since.

Sadly, it is all too easy for those of us who are involved with the church-as-institution to substitute the institution for the person of Christ and to live out of our own strength rather than out of the vital energy supplied by the Spirit who draws from the immeasurable riches of the risen and living One who declares "I am the way, the truth and the life." Perhaps those who think of themselves as spiritual but not religious are longing for an intimate encounter with this love: a love that transforms, heals, and makes all things whole.

While I was Bishop of Chicago, a very active older member of the diocese told me in tears that he loved the Episcopal Church and was deeply upset because in the course of his lifetime it had "changed so." I listened to him and thought: Yes, I am grateful for the Episcopal Church as the particular medium whereby I have encountered Christ. However, I don't love the Episcopal Church. I love the *Lord* of the church.

How ironic it is that I, who have always sat somewhat loose to the church-as-institution, should have found myself its chief pastor and symbolic head. Such is the unpredictability and wry humor of the Holy Spirit.

Not long ago I returned to St. Paul's School to participate in a symposium focused on the future of church-related schools. This occasion provided an opportunity for me to visit the chapel that had been such an important part of my life as a teenager. As chance would have it, a seminary professor who was also part of the conference appeared at my side. She expressed an interest in seeing the chapel, and I offered to be her guide.

During our tour, I took her into the small side chapel known as the Chantry, where in my day the Eucharist was celebrated daily. I pointed out the altar with its copy of a Giotto fresco above it and told her this was where I made my first communion and where I frequently attended the Eucharist during the week. The chapel was furnished with benches and beautifully carved stalls. I pointed to one of the stalls and told her it was where I had always knelt. She paused, looked at me intently, and exclaimed: "This is where your eucharistic theology was formed!" Her words struck a deep chord within me. She was exactly right.

In ways well past my understanding or consciousness, during those early morning Eucharists I came to understand my relation to Christ in terms of mutual abiding—he in me and I in him. As one of the prayers recited over the bread and wine has it: we are "filled with grace and heavenly benediction and made one body with [Christ] that he may dwell in us and we in him." As George Herbert describes it in his poem "The Holy Communion," those "small quantities" of bread and wine had a profound and formative effect on me. Christ had crept by stealth "into my breast" and made his home in my soul's most "subtle rooms." God had drawn me beyond the world I had known into a new and unfamiliar realm of mystery. Like the prophet Jeremiah, God had "enticed" me. As I look back on those early morning encounters with Christ in bread and wine I realize it was then that the Risen Christ, present and active in the sacraments through the working of the Holy Spirit, began to become the ground and focus of my life. While the religious awakening of many occurs through a strong and intense conversion experience, God's way with me has taken the form of a subtle and hidden ongoing evolution. I have had moments when I cried out to God: "So this is what you have been up to—and I wasn't aware of it!" I have no doubt there are more such moments to come.

Of course, an encounter with the Risen Christ is not simply a private experience; it is all wrapped up in the flesh and blood reality of other people as well. The whole notion of the church as the body of Christ in the world, of which we imperfect human beings are limbs and body parts, was made real to me in large measure through the Eucharist. A handful of other boys and faculty members might be present in the chapel on those early mornings at St. Paul's, each for their own reasons, each with their own needs. Because my stall was at the back of the chapel I could take them in and notice their attitudes of prayer or attentiveness and think to myself: *We are united with one another because we are all here to share the same bread and cup.*

Over the years my awareness of the vast diversity among the limbs and members of Christ's body has become ever more real. The singularities, the angularities, the different life experiences that make us who we are find their unity and coherence not in a single point of view or theological opinion but in the ability, in the midst of our differences and singularities, to share the one bread and the one cup. St. Paul in describing the body of Christ declares: "the eye cannot say to the hand I have no need of you." He also says that if all body parts were the same the body would cease to exist. Therefore, difference and distinction and the tensions that often accompany them are integral to the fullness and wholeness of Christ's body. In the midst of doing my part to help the Episcopal Church find its way through the struggles and tensions created by difference, Paul's understanding of the church as a living body comprised of unified difference guided and sustained me.

All of this is by way of explaining that for me, "professionally religious" as I may be, the church is primarily a place of encounter with the risen Christ. In fact, I think it would be fair to say that my whole understanding of the nature of the church began as I prayed in the carved wooden stall those early mornings of my growing-up years.

———⁓———

While I was serving as Bishop of Chicago I was visited one day by the Argentinian-born evangelist Luis Palau, who was calling upon religious leaders of the city in preparation for an evangelical crusade he was soon to conduct. In the course of our conversation, he told me he had been educated in an Anglican school in Argentina. He said that the call he issued during his preaching to accept Christ as one's personal savior was quickly grasped by people who had grown up with the Eucharist because they understand intimacy with Christ in a way many evangelicals, though they use the language of intimacy, do not. As he observed, what could be more intimate than encountering Christ through the act of being fed?

———⁓———

I hear and behold God in every object, yet understand
    God not in the least,
Nor do I understand who there can be more wonderful
    than myself.
Why should I wish to see God better than this day?
I see something of God each hour of the twenty-four, and
    each moment then,
In the faces of men and women I see God, and in my own
    face in the glass,
I find letters from God dropt in the street, and every one
    is sign'd by God's name,
And I leave them where they are, for I know that
    wheresoe'er I go,
Others will punctually come for ever and ever.

               —Walt Whitman, from *Leaves of Grass*

My profession is to always be on the alert to find God in nature, to know his lurking places, to attend all the oratorios, the operas, in nature.
                                        —Henry David Thoreau

Our world is sacramental: that is, it reveals God's presence in everything from the rising of the sun to a tiny insect not larger than a speck of sand. As the Jesuit priest and poet Gerard Manley Hopkins declared, "This world then is word, expression, news of God. Therefore its end, purpose, purport, meaning is God, and its life or work to name and praise God . . ." Hopkins's words echo those of the psalmist who cries out: *The heavens declare the glory of God, and the firmament shows his handiwork* (Psalm 19:1).

In a canticle common to a number of traditions of daily prayer, all creation is bidden to praise God in virtue of its very existence: *Glorify the Lord, all you works of the Lord, praise him and highly exalt him forever.* Creation is then described, beginning with the cosmos, as glorifying and praising the One who called it into being: sun and moon, seasons of the year, all that grows upon the earth, whales, wild beasts, birds, flocks and herds, men and women, spirits and souls of the righteous. Francis of Assisi's "Canticle of the Sun" echoes the same theme: God is praised through the classic four elements of air, water, fire, and earth as well as through all creation.

St. Paul's School was founded by Dr. George C. Shattuck, Jr., a physician from Boston who belonged to the Church of the Advent, a parish that took the sacramental principle seriously, namely, the power of the outward and visible to convey that which is "inward and spiritual." Dr. Shattuck believed that nature possessed such a power, and therefore established his school in the midst of woods and ponds which would provide their own unique instruction. While a student there I knew nothing of his vision; even so, nature spoke to me of mystery and transcendence and the "work of an almighty hand" with much the same power as did the chapel and the Eucharist.

The spacious firmament on high,
With all the blue ethereal sky,
And spangled heavens, a shining frame,
Their great Original proclaim.
Th' unwearied Sun from day to day
Does his Creator's power display;
And publishes to every land
The work of an Almighty hand.

—Joseph Addison

In the Gospel of John, the Word who took on our humanity and came among us in the person of Jesus is described as the agent of creation. "All things came into being through him, and without him not one thing came into being." (John 1:3) Other passages of scripture make the same declaration, as does the Nicene Creed, which is regularly recited across Christian traditions. "We believe in one Lord, Jesus Christ . . . through him all things were made . . ." What this means, therefore, is that all of creation, including human life, is in its very existence, indwelt by Christ. Nothing lies outside his embrace.

Without being aware of it at the time, I was encountering the presence of Christ in the clouds as they soared above the pinnacles of the chapel tower and during my solitary walks through the woods around the school pond. The One who made himself known to his disciples in the breaking of bread was making himself known to me through the beauties of this world.

Some months after I was ordained to the priesthood a salutary warning about the peril of neglecting the contemplative dimension of our lives came my way during my first visit to Mt. Saviour, the Benedictine monastery in Elmira, New York, that became so important to me. This was my first meeting with the prior, Father Damasus Winzen, who, as I have said earlier, became an important guide and friend in the spirit.

An older Roman Catholic priest in Philadelphia had

invited me to join him and a group of newly ordained Roman
Catholic priests of my own age for a retreat. We were all filled
with enthusiasm and progressive theology, and confident we
represented the church of the future. Father Damasus gave us
a series of daily conferences. We were deeply impressed by all
he had to say and also by the fact that he seemed to understand
us and approve of our enthusiasm. What was abundantly clear
to us was that his theology was rooted and grounded in a life
of prayer. "A theologian is one who prays," declared Evagrius
Ponticus many centuries ago. In that sense, Father Damasus was
a true theologian.

On the final day of the retreat he opened his Bible and read
to us from the second chapter of the Book of Revelation. In
the passage the risen Christ addresses the angel—symbolizing
the dominant spirit—of the church in Ephesus. Christ says: "I
know your works, your toil and your endurance . . . that you
are bearing up for the sake of my name, and that you have not
grown weary." At this point Father Damasus paused and we, the
young clergy, looked at one another pleased that he seemed to
know how faithful and hard-working we were. We felt honored
that he had chosen this passage. It seemed a sign of his approval
and encouragement.

But Father Damasus was not finished reading. He continued
with the next verse: "But I have this against you, you have
lost your first love." With that he shut his Bible and fixed us
with a stern but loving gaze. We were stunned and speechless.
In a voice of great authority and intimate knowing he said,
"Gentlemen, you are all newly ordained. You are still in the first
fervor of your ordination. It is a great joy for you to celebrate
the Eucharist, to proclaim God's word and to serve God's
people. But, you may find over time, as demands made upon
you increase, that your fervor diminishes and the things of
God become routine and even burdensome. In that case, you
will have become 'technicians of the sacred' and victims of the
'mechanical church.' That is, you may well continue to function
with competency, but without depth. What you do and say will
be appropriate to your office but it will lack the force and power
of the Holy Spirit. If your ministries are to be life-giving then

you must become an intimate companion of the One who is our life. And, the way to companionship, my dear brothers, is the way of prayer."

I have never forgotten Father Damasus's words, and am profoundly grateful that I heard them at the beginning of my priesthood. It is indeed deep prayer that keeps those of us who are "professionally religious" from getting so caught up in the institution that we lose any sense of the One to whom it points. Being rooted and grounded in prayer liberates us from treating the institution as an idol, and supplies us with a capacity for graced skepticism. This allows us to value the institution without becoming its prisoner or, as Father Damasus put it, a victim of the "mechanical church."

A contemporary Latin American theologian has described one of the results of authentic prayer and availability to the Spirit as "the overturning of idols," that is, the overturning of our self-serving images of God, or of the church, or of ourselves. When I first read this description of prayer I wondered what he meant. I then reflected upon my own life as a person of prayer. Before I was ordained I had a very clear image of the priest I wanted to be: devout, faithful, self-sacrificing, sure, and confident in my grasp of theology. I also had very clear ideas about what the church ought to be in terms of its priorities, its witness, and its liturgical life.

What I did not realize at the time was that my images of priestly life and the church were more the product of my imagination and ego's need for security than they were the work of the Holy Spirit, who—as Jesus tells us—blows freely where the Spirit chooses. Over the years these idols have been overturned, not once but again and again. And I have had to acknowledge that I am being shaped by the Holy Spirit in ways that exceed my immediate grasp. My earlier narrow understanding of the church, "that wonderful and sacred mystery," as one of the Collects in the Episcopal Church's liturgy declares, has been replaced by an enlarged vision. I have become more able to see the church not as something fixed and static but as a "spiritual house" constantly under construction, as we are told in the First Letter of Peter. I have become more able to see the church, and indeed myself, as growing toward maturity in Christ.

> *Prayer is an availability to love on every level of our being.*
> —Dom John Main

> *Prayer is responding to God, by thought and by deeds, with or without words . . . Christian prayer is response to God the Father, through Jesus Christ, in the power of the Holy Spirit.*   —The Book of Common Prayer

Prayer, and what it means to pray, can be variously understood. One common understanding is that prayer is a discipline or activity we initiate ourselves, much as we might practice the piano or maintain an exercise routine. If, however, we understand prayer as an energy that is as fundamental and as intimate to us as our own breath, new possibilities open. The question becomes: how do I collaborate with that energy and give it space within me? How can I cultivate this dimension of myself? What might then emerge?

Over the years my understanding of what it means to pray has expanded and changed greatly. When I was confirmed as a teenager and learning to pray with the little book of prayers I had been given, I understood prayer as *my* activity—a discipline and a duty necessary to attract God's attention. I felt that if I was sufficiently filled with fervor I would be heard.

Looking back, I must admit that my surfeit of devotion led less to a sense of relationship with God and more to overweening pride and satisfaction. Like St. Paul, as he tells us in his Letter to the Galatians, I was "far more zealous" than my contemporaries. Perhaps, even more to the satisfaction of my ego, I had gone beyond most of the priests on the faculty in the rigors of my discipline. Now I can see that in my early efforts to pray my adherence to very set forms and categories of prayer was the Spirit teaching me to pray, step-by-step. It was not that my efforts were insincere or false, but they were quite self-focused and immature. Paul talks about our needing spiritual milk before we are able to digest solid food as we grow spiritually. Our ways of praying evolve over time as the Spirit deepens and matures our capacity for prayer. Our set forms and discreet acts of prayer open the way to a natural sensibility we might call "prayerfulness." Father Richard Meux Benson, the founder of the Society of Saint John the Evangelist, once observed, "Our role in prayer is not to try to raise ourselves to God by the violence of natural effort, but to surrender, to cooperate in the movement by which the Holy Spirit rises to the Father."

At some point in my early struggles to be prayerful I happened upon a passage in the Letter to the Romans in which St. Paul tells us: "Likewise the Spirit helps us in our weakness; for we do not know how to pray as we ought, but that very Spirit intercedes with sighs too deep for words. And God, who searches the heart, knows what is the mind of the Spirit, because the Spirit intercedes for the saints according to the will of God." (Romans 8:26–27)

What an overwhelming relief it is to be told by none other than St. Paul himself that we don't know how to pray as we ought. What a sense of liberation. What a deliverance from the burden of believing that it is up to us to achieve success in prayer. How comforting it is to have Paul tell us that even he found himself dumbstruck and inadequate in the face of knowing how to respond to God's overwhelming mystery. We pray always out of our weakness, and it is the Spirit who can use even our sighs and yearnings to draw us into companionship with Christ. Even our inability to pray to our own satisfaction can be an invitation to pass beyond self-judgment and to yield our poverty in prayer to the Spirit who prays continually within us.

George Herbert, in the cascading metaphors of his poem "Prayer (I)", describes prayer as "God's breath in man returning to its birth." Rather than understanding prayer as something extraordinary and unusual, the poet, and St. Paul as well, understood prayer as a fundamental dimension of our humanity. Prayer is as natural to us as breathing. As Christ revealed to Dame Julian of Norwich, a great English mystic of the fifteenth century, "I am the ground of your beseeching." In other words, she was being told that Christ himself was the origin of her prayer. And prayer, she tells us, makes us one with God.

———————

There is a verse in Psalm 27 in which the psalmist declares: "You [God] speak in my heart and say, 'Seek my face.'" The psalmist replies: "Your face, Lord, will I seek." This verse tells us that the Spirit in various ways is constantly saying—*Seek my face, seek my face*—and is drawing us beyond ourselves into the fathomless depths of the mystery of God.

———————

Prayer requires what the French Roman Catholic philosopher Gabriel Marcel describes as "availability." When we are available our defenses are down and we are freed from our usual distractions and preoccupations. Our hearts and minds are open to the free-ranging motions of the Spirit who moves within the depths of our own spirits drawing us into an ever-deepening communion with God in Christ.

Availability to God's mystery simply means that we are open to the power of the Spirit praying within us and bringing to our consciousness those things of which we need to be aware. Our ongoing companionship with Christ, intentionally supported by formal and informal practices of prayer, sensitizes us such that we are increasingly available to the motions of the Spirit. Thus, the Spirit works within our own spirit in a connatural way. It is not that we hear a voice from heaven giving advice or an answer, but rather that we find ourselves impelled to act spontaneously and with self-forgetfulness. Our prayer prepares us to be vehicles for the Holy Spirit, beyond our imagining.

Our companionship with Christ enables Christ's Spirit to work in us and through us as situations arise. For example, we might feel calm and confident under circumstances that in anticipation terrify us. Or, we might find ourselves able to speak truth at a time when we are tempted to remain silent. As well, at times when we feel overwhelmed by anxiety, we may be suddenly infused with a sense of confidence and interior peace. Maybe we hear the still, small voice of the Spirit saying *all shall be well*, even though we don't know how or when. In such moments we realize that it is not us, but the Spirit of Christ working within us at the heart of our prayer.

Such availability is often not deliberately chosen but thrust upon us by circumstance. We suddenly find ourselves poor, bereft, defenseless. Yet, paradoxically, at such moments we often come in touch with a force within us that we had not previously known. This was the experience of Mihajalo Mihajlov, a prominent dissident in the former Yugoslavia who was jailed for seven years during the Cold War era. In an article smuggled out of prison in 1976, entitled "The Mystical Experience of the Loss of Freedom," he wrote: "In the depths of the human soul there dwells an unexplained force which is stronger—and not only symbolically, but empirically stronger—than all outward forces of oppression and destruction, however invincible they may seem." He continues, "the fate of men is not decided by earthly powers, by outward, physical forces, but only by the mystical power which from time immemorial has been called 'God,' and whose relationship to man seems to depend on man's relationship to his inner voice."

———

"Pray simply," Macarius of Optina, a nineteenth-century Russian teacher of prayer, advises us. "Do not expect to find in your heart any remarkable gift of prayer. Consider yourself unworthy of it. Then you will find peace. Use the empty, dry coldness of your prayer as food for your humility. Repeat constantly 'I am not worthy, Lord, I am not worthy!' But say it calmly, without agitation. This humble prayer will be accepted by God."

The terms upon which God accepts our prayer are not for us to decide, nor is the fruit of our prayer for us to determine. God's imagination and larger purposes exceed all that we can ask or imagine. What a consolation it is that, without our being aware of it, the fruit of the Spirit can grow within us. Paul describes this fruit as love, joy, peace, patience, kindness, generosity, faithfulness, gentleness, and self-control. Taken together these qualities represent one reality, namely the character of Christ.

Above all, the Spirit praying within us expands our hearts and transfigures them with Christ's own love and compassion, thereby rendering them merciful and able to embrace all things.

———————

In the Book of Common Prayer there is "An Outline of the Faith" that includes a list of "the principal kinds of prayer." They are adoration, praise, thanksgiving, penitence, oblation, intercession, and petition. If you turn to the Internet you will find other lists as well, including one that names "The Top Five Types of Prayer." My difficulty with any such lists is that instead of leading us more deeply into the mystery of prayer, they can become a holy "to-do list" for which we hold ourselves responsible and of which we consider ourselves to be the initiating force. This can lead so easily to a kind of anxious self-preoccupation. Though such lists can be helpful in our cooperation with the motions of the Spirit, at a deeper level they point to the fact that the Spirit prays within us in a variety of ways.

———————

> *Pray as you can, and do not try to pray as you can't. Take*
> *yourself as you find yourself, and start from that.*
> —Dom John Chapman

There are times when patterns of prayer or devotional practices that have been fruitful and life-giving seem to collapse and leave us in places of dryness and desolation. We become discouraged in our efforts to pray and hear a voice of judgment within ourselves telling us: *You are not praying properly. Your prayer is inadequate. Your prayer is superficial.*

At such times, we might seek to be more fervent in our prayer and blame ourselves for what seems to be a sense of God's absence. Because prayer is the work of the Holy Spirit conforming us to the image of Christ, it involves a sometimes-painful purification of our desires, especially our desire to be proficient in our prayer. In such moments we need to remember that our preoccupation with the quality and effectiveness of our prayer can be the work of the evil one masquerading as an angel of light.

At such times God may be leading us beyond the consolations we have known into a place of deeper intimacy that can only be entered through our willingness to be patient and to endure, trusting in God's mercy alone. It is precisely at the point when we think we have mastered the "art of praying" that the bottom may fall out, and our carefully constructed spiritual disciplines seem to crumble. At such times, we may find ourselves confronted by a sense of inadequacy, failure, and—above all—spiritual poverty. Then, as we stand defenseless before God, God's grace can break in and have its way with us. Our first reaction, however, may be to offset our sense of failure by trying to exert more fervor. This usually fails to work and simply imprisons us more and more in frustration with ourselves in the face of our seeming inadequacy.

During the "dark night of the soul," as so eloquently described by St. John of the Cross, we may feel that our prayer is useless and without fruit. And, yet, God may be working secretly within us. The hidden activity of the Spirit produces its own fruit. Our very willingness to surrender our poverty in prayer to the mercy of God opens the way for God to shape and mold us, not according to our own hopes and aspirations but according to the Divine desire and intention.

"The purpose of prayer is not the same as the purpose of speech. The purpose of speech is to inform; the purpose of prayer is to partake." These are the words of the late Rabbi Abraham Joshua Heschel, a Jewish teacher of prayer. The partaking of which Rabbi Heschel speaks is our partaking in God's own life because we have been made in God's image and likeness.

One of the Holy Spirit's wily ways is to entice us to move beyond asking God to act into acting ourselves. Here is an example. Over the years at moments of frustration I have found that physical activity can dissipate negative energy. In the summer I take my scythe out to a meadow and cut down weeds. At other seasons I might wield a hot iron against damp linen napkins. On one occasion while I was working away, iron in hand, a certain bishop came suddenly and unexpectedly to mind, and with him the awareness that his wife was suffering from cancer. As I continued to iron I held them both prayerfully in mind only to hear a still small voice within me tell me to call him up and find out how his wife was doing. I then had a debate with myself. Would such an unexpected call be an imposition, or come at a bad moment? Wasn't I simply meant to pray for them? Part of me hoped for a resounding yes in answer. However, I did not hear such a yes and continued to feel the urgency to telephone. I succumbed, and called. The bishop answered the phone. I told him he had suddenly come to mind and I wondered how his wife was doing. He told me she was not doing well, and I assured him of my concern and my prayers. Some months later we were together at a meeting and he took me aside and said: "You have no idea how much your call meant to me. At that particular moment I felt very alone in a dark place." Fortunately, I had not had any idea, and had to acknowledge to myself that the Spirit, praying within me, had decided—against my initial resistance—to make me the bearer of a consoling word. I guess this tells us that prayer can be dangerous, leading us beyond word into action.

Amazing Grace

> *The grace of our Lord Jesus Christ, the love of God, and*
> *the communion of the Holy Spirit be with all of you.*
> —2 Corinthians 13:14

Though I have prayed these words countless times, grace, love, and communion are actually three aspects of one reality. Just as the three Persons of the Trinity—Father, Son, and Spirit— always act together in perfect unity, so, too, grace, love, and communion are intimately related. People have sometimes said to me that they pray to the Father but not to Jesus, or that they are drawn to the Holy Spirit but not to the Father. I point out that all three together constitute one Divine reality, though our focus may be on the Father, the Son, or the Holy Spirit. In other words, as I have said somewhat jokingly, if you get one you get them all. That is, God's self-gift may be experienced as grace, as love, or as communion.

Grace, however, is not some kind of disembodied energy that gets poured into our souls, but rather a way of describing God's love for us. And grace, this "love energy," if you will, establishes and expresses itself in a reciprocal relationship of love—that is, in communion.

It has become clear to me over the years that God's profligate and unbounded love for us is reflected in God's desire to be in communion with us. And, as God's love finds a home within us, it enlivens us and provokes us to deeds of love, which become our answering yes. Simply put, grace is God's loving presence at work in our lives and it contains within it the invitation to respond. Because love is an energy, a dynamic force, it must express itself in some form or it ceases to be love.

Paul tells us in the Letter to the Romans that the love of God is poured into our hearts through the Holy Spirit. However, God's love for us is not experienced as a possession we can tuck away and pull out from time to time to appreciate. Rather, God's love poured into our hearts is reflected in our capacity to love. In other words, God's love poured into our hearts becomes the ground of our own loving. Over time, our capacity to love and the patterns of our loving are enabled and increased by the power of God's love working within us. The Spirit who pours God's love into our hearts draws close to our own spirits and enables our spirits to expand and to express themselves in deeds and words of love.

What a consolation it is to remind ourselves that the Holy Spirit is always present. It is not as if we had to import something into our lives. The Spirit is already there. We simply need to be aware of that loving presence. However, it is also the case that we are not always present to the Holy Spirit because of the "dullness of our blinded sight," as a hymn has it. And, by not having eyes to see, or ears to hear, we miss the more subtle movements of the Spirit, and its deeper presence within the depths of our own spirits.

We might assume it would be easier to sense the Divine presence when things are going well. My experience has been that the presence of the Spirit can be more acute when things are not going well, when we hit a rough patch. At such times, paradoxically, we may become aware of a deep sense of being companioned in a way that "passes all understanding."

The grace of the Holy Spirit can work in ways so subtle we are not even aware of it at the time. Perhaps this is the way it should be. We are told in the Book of Exodus that when Moses came down from Mt. Sinai after his encounter with God he did not know that the skin of his face shone because he had been talking with God. "When Aaron and all the Israelites saw Moses, the skin of his face was shining and they were afraid to come near him." Can you imagine how lethal we would be if we were aware of God's activity within us and congratulated ourselves because we had been the recipients of so great a gift? God's activity within us is not meant to provoke in us a kind of ego gratification because we have been so greatly favored by the Divine radiance. Rather, it is to be lived out humbly in self-gift and love.

Because love renews our minds and transforms our consciousness we find ourselves seeing others and the world around us with "undistorted sight" and are thereby drawn toward them. We see them somewhat as God sees them: that is with reverence and compassion. This experience of seeing works within us an acute awareness of a relation between us and others that is nothing less than "the communion of the Holy Spirit."

Here I am put in mind of a remarkable conversation that occurred in 1831 between a Russian landowner and businessman, Nicholas Motovilov, and St. Seraphim of Sarov, who was renowned for his holiness and acute spiritual insight. The conversation was included in the memoirs of Motovilov. He recounted that he had made his way to the forest hermitage in which Seraphim spent the last twenty-five years of his life. In a forest glade, surrounded by falling snow, Motovilov asked Seraphim: "How can I know I am in the Holy Spirit?"

Motovilov recounts that "then Father Seraphim took me very firmly by the shoulders and said: 'we are both in the Spirit of God now, my son. Why don't you look at me?' I replied 'I cannot look, Father, because your eyes are flashing like lightning. Your face has become brighter than the sun, and my eyes ache with pain.'"

Motovilov goes on to say: "Imagine in the center of the sun, in the dazzling light of its midday rays, the face of a man talking to you."

Seraphim then told Motovilov: "Now you yourself have become as bright as I am. You too are now in the fullness of God's Spirit; otherwise you would not be able to see me as I am."

Motovilov's account may seem extravagant and beyond belief, yet, I have had encounters with people across the years who have been in some sense "luminous" and whose very presence was a manifestation of the power of the Spirit to inhabit our humanity and make our words, our actions, our very being signs of God's presence. I remember taking communion on Christmas Day to a young physician who was dying of leukemia. I'd come to know him as he lived through the excruciating experience, which was particularly difficult for him as he was a hematologist and had a heightened awareness of the likely course of the disease.

I remember bending over his hospital bed. As I offered him the eucharistic bread, I was startled by the radiance and joy that transfigured his ravaged face. It was a complete contradiction to his physical state. He cried out, "This is the most wonderful gift I could possibly have!" I was overwhelmed and suddenly aware that, though I was offering him Christ in the eucharistic bread, I was seeing Christ in the dying man before me. It was a very intense exchange of love—Christ's love present in both of us and revealed in that sacramental encounter. Indeed, both of us were in the Holy Spirit.

As I prepared to leave he awkwardly took my hand and kissed

it, and then, realizing how impulsive this action had been, he quickly said, "You're my Pope, and that's why I kissed your ring." There was no ring. *No, no, John,* I thought. *You're not going to get away with this.* I leaned over the bed and kissed him on the forehead. Our eyes met and we both knew something profound had occurred: Christ was in our midst, luminous in John's face. I wonder now if I might have appeared luminous as well.

When the Spirit dwells within a person, from the moment that person has become prayer; the Spirit never leaves them. For the Spirit himself never ceases to pray within us. Whether we are asleep or awake, from then on prayer never departs from our soul. Whether we are eating or drinking or sleeping or whatever else we may be doing, even if we are in the deepest of sleeps, the incense of prayer is rising without effort in our heart. Prayer never again deserts us. In every moment of our life, even when it appears to have ceased, prayer is secretly at work within us continuously.
    —Isaac of Syria, from the *Ascetical Treatises*

A Morning Offering

Lord, grant me to greet the coming day in peace.
Help me to rely on your holy will.
In every hour of the day reveal your will to me.
Bless my dealings with all who surround me.
Teach me to treat all that comes to me throughout the day
    with peace of soul
    and with the firm belief that your will governs all.
Guide my words and deeds, my thoughts and feelings.
Teach me to act firmly and wisely
    without embittering or embarrassing others.

> *Give me the strength to bear the fatigue of the coming day*
> *with all that it shall bring.*
> *Direct my will. Teach me to pray. Pray yourself in me.*
> *Amen.*
> —Philaret,
> Metropolitan of Moscow (1826–1867)

During the years Philaret served as Metropolitan, he was called upon to exercise significant diplomatic skills in dealing with tense relations between church and state. As well, he sought to instill in his people a deeper and more mature faith, and to that end produced a catechism that has remained influential in Russia and beyond for nearly two hundred years. In 1995 the Russian Orthodox Church, in recognition of his significance and many gifts, declared Philaret a saint and established November 19 as his feast day.

I first came across his "Morning Offering" during my years as Presiding Bishop. I suppose I was drawn to it because I, like Philaret, had oversight of an ecclesial community and was confronted day-by-day with the stresses and strains associated with church leadership—or leadership of any sort for that matter. On many mornings, I would enter into the new day asking myself how I could best deal with what might lie ahead. Philaret's prayer continues to be important to me and to draw forth my own reflections.

> *Lord, grant me to greet the coming day in peace.*

I pray that I may not superimpose upon the day, even before it unfolds, anxieties or negative anticipations, but rather that I am able to enter into it in a focused state of trust and receptivity.

> *Help me to rely on your holy will.*
> *In every hour of the day reveal your will to me.*
> *Teach me to treat all that comes to me throughout the day*
> *with peace of soul*
> *and with the firm belief that your will governs all.*

What do we mean when we talk about "God's will"? Is it a divine agenda? A five-point plan? Not at all. The Greek word for "will" as it appears in the New Testament has several meanings, one of which is to "feel affection for." Doing God's will, therefore, is less about obeying an order and more a response to the joy of being loved. I am so aware as a parent that my *will* for my children is not that they submit to my list of *oughts* and *shoulds* and *musts,* but that they go well in their lives. My love and care for them is constant. And, I accept the potential anguish that their choices may not always be in accord with what I think would be best. In fact, my will for them is that they may grow and flourish in ways that may well exceed, and possibly contradict, my own desires and imaginings.

I pray that I may sit lightly with my own expectations and make space for new insights or ways of seeing that may come from God's desire rather than my own. This fundamental orientation needs to be renewed again and again during the day. Sometimes I start the day praying for largeness of spirit only to find that several hours later I am constricted by anger or judgment. My desire to be one with God's desire needs to be renewed in the midst of circumstances that may seem difficult or overwhelming.

> *Guide my words and deeds, my thoughts and feelings.*
> *Teach me to act firmly and wisely*
> *without embittering or embarrassing others.*

I realize that Christ is present in those who cross my path each day. I must admit, however, that sometimes that presence is deeply hidden and hard to recognize.

I pray for freedom to see as God sees, and not to become entrapped in my biases or predetermined views of those I will encounter. My actions need to be informed by the Spirit of truth who works in us the mind of Christ. Since the Spirit of truth also pours God's love into our hearts, speaking the truth involves love. Truth may be painful to receive but when it is infused by love it has a greater possibility of being accepted without bitterness or embarrassment.

Give me the strength to bear the fatigue of the coming
day with all that it shall bring.

I hear in these words the need to accept the limits of my own humanity and to realize that I may well grow weary. I find it consoling that St. Philaret acknowledged before God the limits of his own strength. I pray always to rely on God's grace and to avoid the temptation to exceed it by indulging in messianic fantasies about my own abilities and endurance.

Direct my will. Teach me to pray. Pray yourself in me.

With these words I am inviting Christ to reconcile my hopes and desires with Christ's own, and to make his prayer of loving availability to God's desire the ground of my own prayer. I also acknowledge that I will become preoccupied in the course of the day, and—inevitably—lose my bearings. Rather than judging myself at such moments as deficient or unfaithful, I find rest in the fact that the Spirit of Christ prays within me continuously below the level of my own consciousness.

Finding Our Way
in a Sea of Choices

Oh dear Lord, three things I pray . . .
To see thee more clearly,
Love thee more dearly,
Follow thee more nearly,
Day by day

—From the musical *Godspell*,
based on a prayer
by St. Richard of Chichester

Discernment: The ability to see and understand people,
things or situations intelligently and clearly.

—Merriam-Webster Dictionary

Teach me the way I should go . . .   —Psalm 143:8

Every day we are confronted by a variety of choices and possibilities. *Shall I do this or do that? Shall I go or stay? Shall I yield to the desire that is flooding my imagination and urging me to "go with the flow," or should I resist and submit it to scrutiny?*

As well, our state of mind colors our perceptions. *Am I feeling overwhelmed and a little burned out? Am I ignoring my own deepest longings? Am I moved by feelings of forgiveness, or revenge, in responding to someone who has offended me? Am I acting out of love or fear or self-protection? What emotions and pre-judgments are at work in me? Am I feeling anxious, angry, jealous, or am I craving recognition or affirmation? Am I by nature trusting or suspicious?*

In large measure our attitudes and daily decisions, insignificant and momentous, determine who we are. They can open and expand our consciousness, making us ever more our truest selves, or they can pinch our spirits and turn us inward.

117

Our capacity for awareness—being able to see with undistorted sight—is comprised of many forces, cultural and otherwise, all of which shape and form us and thereby constitute what we perceive as reality. Questionable patterns of thought and behavior can become so deeply embedded in our consciousness that they escape detection and are mistaken for unassailable truth. This state of unawareness can lead to negative consequences in the guise of virtue, patriotism, or orthodoxy.

Related to this is the question of time, a limited resource. We cannot do everything, and the constraints of time and the question of how we spend it are ever with us. For example, I am aware of the ever-seductive possibilities offered by the Internet. Not long ago I observed something that has become so commonplace it is part of our cultural humor. Away on a trip, I was eating alone at a restaurant in Richmond, Virginia, when a family of six sat down at the next table. As soon as they made their meal choices the parents, setting the example, whipped out their cell phones. They were quickly followed by three of the four children. The fourth sat sullenly for a few minutes and then she succumbed to what had become the solo activity of six seemingly unrelated people. The food arrived and each one ate in silence, their faces illumined by the light of the phone still in hand. In this case, the choice made was to share a table while each remained immured in a private world, rather than entering into an experience of shared conviviality. As I observed them, all I could think was that an opportunity had been missed, never to be recovered.

Our choices about how we spend time are a matter of stewardship. In this season of my life the use of my twenty-four hours a day is no longer determined by my formal employment. It is largely up to me to determine how I will deploy this limited resource. In the absence of "a job" almost anything can become the primary focus of my attention, while more important or demanding tasks might be left unattended.

Not long ago I was invited to give a talk on the spirituality of St. Francis of Assisi. Given the role of St. Francis in my own life I was happy to accept the invitation. In the course of my preparation, I thought about the Giotto frescos in the Basilica where Francis is buried. Turning to the Internet, I found out that I could have a fresh look and a virtual tour. This opened the way to other possibilities for adventures in Assisi, including a visit to the Cathedral of San Rufino containing the font where Francis was baptized. My mood became increasingly Italian and so I set off for further exploration of the delights of the Province of Perugia. Such wandering left me hungry and I indulged in a quick look at restaurant menus with distracting advertising sidebars along the way, including "tips for a flat stomach." By this time, the excursion had taken more than an hour and the talk had progressed no further.

"Teach me the way that I should go," prays the psalmist. The answer to this prayer seldom seems to fall from the sky. Instead, we must sort and sift possibilities and choices, the various words and events that present themselves to us. Our lifelong task is seeking to know God's desire for us and our full flourishing, and how we are meant to participate in God's continuing work of healing and reconciliation in this fragile and wounded world. This work involves collaboration between our spirit and the Holy Spirit: the Spirit of truth who, according to Jesus, guides us into all truth. Across the centuries men and women have employed disciplines and practices to grow in awareness of God's fathomless mystery and the deep truth of who they are and are called to be. These disciplines and practices teach us about God and ourselves, about the interplay of light and darkness, about the foibles of being human and, above all, about the wild and unrestrained love and compassion of Christ our Teacher, who is the truth.

Since my school days at St. Paul's and my membership in the Servants of Christ the King I have had a rule of life; that is, a pattern of daily practice that has grounded me and helped me to be open to God's word. "Oh, that today you would harken to his voice!" Thus declares the psalmist in Psalm 95, which since the early days of the church has been chanted as each day begins.

The term "rule" may sound somewhat stark and legalistic but

what it points to is simply a recurring rhythm of spiritual practice that attunes our interior ear to the many ways the Lord speaks daily to our hearts and minds and impels us to be ministers of his reconciling love. The word comes from the Latin *regula*, from which we get the word "regulate": that is, to order in such a way that a thing may perform or function in accord with its nature or purpose. A rule of life, therefore, seeks to order the various dimensions of our lives in such a way that we may "function" as the persons we, in God's eyes, are called to be.

For me, having a rule of life means my daily practice is not dependent on my mood. I have something to set me right when I am preoccupied or disconsolate and not at all eager to hear God's voice. My present rule of life is derived from that of a monastic community. Many communities invite men and women to be associated with them by following a rule of life that reflects the character of that community. Though rules vary according to the character of the community, they usually include daily prayer, corporate worship, study, self-care, stewardship, and service. Taking on an existing and tested rule saves us from creating some extravagant and overreaching rule of our own that would probably be impossible to keep or, worse, be an exercise in ego inflation. Taking on an existing rule means being associated with others engaged daily in the same pattern of practice. Knowing I am joined with others in a shared spiritual endeavor is an encouragement at times when my mood or the daily demands threaten to draw me off in other directions.

Here I note that neuroscience tells us when something is repeated enough times our brain cells adjust and it becomes a habit. My sense is that my brain has now—over all these years— embedded my rule of life and, in this respect, I have become a "creature of habit." Good habits can sustain us and keep us grounded. At the mundane level, isn't it good that we don't have to spend time wondering if we ought to brush our teeth? The "quotidian round" is pretty well established by the time we move beyond childhood. In my own case I know I am very well served by ordered patterns of prayer and participation in the sacramental life of the church.

Unawareness is the root of all evil.

This rather startling statement comes from the desert tradition of the fourth century. The harsh and forbidding landscape and silence of the wilderness wastes of Egypt and Palestine became the setting in which stalwart and Spirit-driven men and women explored the inner landscape of their hearts and the interplay of various spirits: those of light and darkness, truth and self-deception, and the raging demons of their own unmasked desires. Alone with God, and freed from all the distractions afforded by life in the world, they came to know themselves naked before the great Mystery of God. "In the desert the air is purer, the sky is more open, and God is closer," observed Origen, a third-century ascetic and theologian. The fruit of their labor and the work of the Spirit was a purification of heart and mind. This produced a heightened quality of awareness that allowed them to recognize how our ability to see accurately is compromised by the attitudes, opinions, and cultural norms that affect our inner landscape.

On the other hand, unawareness allows the spirits of disorder and untruth to ensnare us. Negative assumptions and points of view about ourselves and the "other" become an unconscious background and are woven into a complex web of social, cultural, and political attitudes and perspectives. Racism and any number of other "-isms" might well fall into this category. Over time, these "realities" can be perceived simply as right and true. Such disordered patterns of thought can be so deeply embedded in our own personal and collective psyches that their uncovering may well cause anger and resistance. The cost of relinquishing the dark comfort and security of our attitudes, and all that flows from them, is tantamount to a kind of death. As the old collapses, we find ourselves in a new and uncertain space that can move us either backwards in an attempt to recover the former security of our imagined world, or open us to a yet-to-be-revealed new way of perceiving and being.

There are those for whom the idea of anyone who is not a white male serving as President of the United States or CEO of a major corporation is an aberration and a shock to their worldview. In my own life I think about how I once blithely assumed it was an immutable truth that only men could be priests.

When I became a bishop, at the urging of a wise colleague I went to a psychotherapist to explore how my family of origin and my upbringing affected my exercise of oversight and leadership. The experience was eye-opening. I discovered that some attitudes I unthinkingly considered as generally normative were quite particular to me, and had been determined by what I had been taught or observed and experienced as a child. Because of my father's alcoholism and the domestic chaos it produced, I often looked through the lens of "catastrophic fantasy"—that is, I might anticipate the worst when faced with threatening or complex situations. To have this tendency flushed out of hiding and named was immensely helpful and liberating. It still lurks in my consciousness, but it has none of its old power and no longer conditions my responses without me recognizing its distorting presence.

Do not believe every spirit, test the spirits to see whether they are from God; for many false prophets have gone out into the world.   —1 John 4:1

As Gerard Manley Hopkins has said, the world is word, expression, news of God. Our task then is to sort and sift the various words and events that present themselves to us, and to find in this jumble what we might call the authentic word meant for us. This work of discernment is a lifelong, ongoing process as we remain in dialogue with ourselves about our actions and choices, asking if they seem to point toward the full flourishing God desires for us and for others. We are obliged, also, daily to discern how best to respond to all that life sets before us, bidden and unbidden. This may seem arduous when lined out in this fashion. However, it is actually what we do every day, whether we name it as such or not.

Our work of discernment is complicated by the fact that our ability to see as God sees is, as I have said, compromised and occluded by our attitudes and opinions, and the various distorting lenses through which we view the world and ourselves within it. As well, we are all shaped for good or ill by the social and cultural forces that we accept, largely without scrutiny, simply as reality and as "the way things are." All this comes into play when we try to make choices or responses in concert with the "Spirit of truth," so named by Jesus.

Christians in the early centuries took very seriously the charge in the First Letter of John to test the spirits. In the fourth century, Evagrius Ponticus, a noted theologian and desert monastic, identified eight patterns of thought (*logismoi*). They are gluttony, lust, avarice, sadness, anger, acedia, vainglory, and pride. In the West they morphed into the Seven Deadly Sins as pride and vainglory became one. Evagrius did not see the eight as sins in themselves, but rather doorways to sin if undetected and allowed to pervade our consciousness.

It is useful to imagine these as eight lenses through which we might look at the world. We may naively assume we have an accurate and unbiased view when, in actuality, what we see is colored by our lens, which can distort our response. If we are looking through a lens of anger, we may see the world with a hostility that makes us defensive and constantly on guard. If avarice is our lens, our desire to possess can possess us and determine our choices and worldview.

It is worth noting too that the unfolding of these affectivities—these eight patterns of thought—occurs largely in the imagination. We play out certain scenarios. I imagine myself preaching. Moved by pride and vainglory I then picture grateful members of the congregation grasping my hand and with eager voices thanking me for my wisdom and insight. Or, in the case of anger, I imagine ways I might "return the favor" to someone I think has wronged me. Lust also resides in the imagination, as we see so clearly from the barrage of provocation to which we are daily exposed. More subtle is acedia, also called the noonday demon, which Evagrius describes as a kind of listlessness and boredom and a bitterness of soul that immobilizes us on a sea of dissatisfaction.

The eighteenth-century English mystic William Law speaks of befriending the "dark guest," or what we might call the shadow dimensions of our humanity that lurk within us. Evagrius's categories help us identify the various ways the dark guest can show up within our imagination and consciousness. Befriending the different manifestations of the dark guest means that, rather than suppressing or denying the presence of these various states, we bring them to full awareness and acknowledge them as part of who we are. This very acknowledgment can loosen their hold upon us and expose the subtle ways they move within us, hoping not to be detected. Keeping the dark guest hidden and secret gives it power over us. Acknowledging its presence, not just to ourselves but to a wise and mature spiritual friend, confessor, or therapist, as humbling as it may be, can be immensely freeing and greatly reduce the shadow's power.

The counsel in the First Letter of John, to "test the spirits," brings to mind other insights from scripture. In the Gospel of John, Jesus describes Satan as the "father of lies" and declares, "Lying is his nature." That is, untruth in any form is a manifestation of evil. Here I think of our way of colluding with untruth by accepting as true a rumor, usually negative, without trying to determine its validity simply because it supports our already formed opinion or point of view.

Over time seemingly innocent comments or jokes that support stereotyping or demeaning particular persons or groups can very easily lead us further and further into disparagement and hostility, thereby rendering our distorted perceptions as true. This can happen without our even noticing it and the end result is that a lie becomes accepted as the truth.

One of the most horrifying examples of this capacity for untruth was the Holocaust. In the case of Nazi Germany, a bias, a disdain and prejudice, advanced step-by-step until it became a carefully calculated plan for mass extermination. The fact that the commandant of an extermination camp could enjoy an idyllic life with his family on one side of the garden wall while atrocity beyond imagining occurred on the other side is a stark example of how human awareness can be subverted by evil.

Another insight from scripture comes from the Second Letter

to the Corinthians in which Paul tells us "Satan disguises himself as an angel of light." There are times when we are overtaken by a vision of something, often cosmic in scope, of some greater good. We delight in imagining the possibilities before us, and we see ourselves accomplishing great deeds. Where does this urge come from? Is it a genuine invitation from the Spirit, or is it the fruit of self-generated heroism: an ego projection of an idealized self? If it is the latter, we may either exceed our capacity to carry it out and find ourselves mired in a sense of failure or bitterness of spirit, or so overwhelmed and immobilized by the magnitude of the task looming before us that we fail to undertake something we can achieve because we are in thrall to our grandiose plan. When we are tempted to go beyond what we are able to do, we might call this an "exaggeration of generosity." We picture ourselves dashing forth to save the world when God is calling us to do something more modest, such as having a quiet lunch with a friend experiencing a hard time or volunteering at the local library. Such temptations may come from a lack of awareness of our own human limitations and need for self-care. I often remind myself when faced with this temptation that Jesus, in sharing our humanity, had to accommodate such limitations as the need for rest, for sleep, and time to be alone.

We must be wary of the inner voice that urges us to reach beyond what the Spirit is inviting us to do, and thereby exceed the grace God is actually giving us. Here I remember a priest who had just returned from a very profound retreat experience telling me that he had come away with a strong sense of Christ's invitation to leave his parish and become a missionary in a particularly remote and troubled part of the world. As he described his sense of call with great passion, I remembered that the lay leadership of his parish had recently informed me that he was becoming less and less attentive to the pastoral needs of his flock, and that his preaching was increasingly thin and shallow. "What does your wife think about all this?" I asked. He stopped abruptly and looked surprised. "I haven't asked her," he replied.

"Perhaps you should, since this affects her and your children.

And perhaps," I added, "the deeper invitation from the Lord is to stay put and to be more attentive to the demands of your present situation." He took my words to heart, and a new season of ministry filled with energy and conviction opened for him and his congregation. He had resisted the temptation that came disguised as a "greater good."

———⌢———

"Hands to work and hearts to God." This saying epitomizes the approach of the Shakers, an offshoot of the Quakers, founded in England in the eighteenth century. Several Shaker communities thrived in this country over two hundred years ago, including one in Canterbury, New Hampshire, not far from where Phoebe and I spend our summers. The Shaker approach of "hands to work and hearts to God" led over the years to the production of furniture and tools designed with simplicity of line and usefulness uppermost. Phoebe and I became attracted to Shaker furniture through our acquaintance with the Canterbury Shaker Village, now a museum with a store selling reproductions of the Shaker furniture, some of which has come home with Phoebe and me over the years. One year I discovered a kit that allowed non-Shakers, like me, to assemble their own Shaker reproductions. When our daughter Eliza was eight, I decided I would assemble a child's rocking chair and present it to her for Christmas. I should say here that carpentry and furniture refinishing are not in my skill set. However, the directions that came with the kit made it sound quite simple.

Sometime before Christmas, back home in Pennsylvania, with a great sense of anticipation for what I was about to achieve, I successfully assembled the chair and prepared for the next step of finishing the wood. Though the kit included sandpaper and instructions for its use, I decided that even this very fine sandpaper would not allow me to reach Shaker perfection, so I went out and bought 000 steel wool, no doubt humming all the while the old Shaker tune "Simple Gifts": "Tis the gift to be simple . . ."

I carefully burnished the wood with the 000 steel wool and then applied the appropriate stain. The next step would be applying polyurethane to preserve it all and give it a sheen. This didn't seem sufficient to me. I decided that for the chair to be truly authentic I would eschew such a thing as modern polyurethane and use shellac instead. As the chair was drying I noticed that the shellac had puddled on one of the arms of the chair. This was not the perfect Shaker chair I had set out to make! Now, I was furious at myself. How could I give Eliza such an imperfect and un-Shaker-like chair? I decided that indeed I would not. Instead, I would take it with me to New Hampshire in the summer and there, in the midst of the Shaker ethos, strip it and start over.

Summer came, the chair traveled to New Hampshire with us, and with the greatest possible care I applied shellac once again while Eliza watched with interest. The arms were now perfect; however, a careful look at the back slats revealed puddled shellac. Again, the chair was imperfect. Of course, I was very angry and frustrated at my ineptitude. Eliza, observing all of this through her eight-year-old eyes, said solemnly: "Dad, I don't even want that chair." I protested, "If it's the last thing I do you are going to have this chair, and the next time it will be right!"

That evening the family dinner was a dramatic occasion. I sat and fumed visibly as a display of my anger at myself, while Phoebe, Hannah, and Eliza looked at me, one another, and colluded in rolling their eyes as if to say: "Oh Dad . . ."

This drove me deeper into my desolation. When dinner ended I went off by myself and decided to place the whole situation in the context of prayer. I did this with some resistance, as there was a dark pleasure in holding on to the negative feelings. However, I laid it all before the Lord: the chair, the shellac, my failure, my ineptitude—and suddenly I heard within my mind a voice saying: "Frank, you are not a Shaker."

With that I was released. Of course not. I am *not* a Shaker. In taking on what had started as a generous impulse, my expectations had leapt well beyond my actual capabilities. The grace of the generous impulse has been exceeded, and rather than bringing forth a happy conclusion, it had become an occasion for anger and negativity. I saw then that Satan had been masquerading as an angel of light: tempting me under the form of something good but then urging me to go beyond what I could competently do, which served to defeat the original generous impulse.

With my release from this exaggeration of generosity I was able to weave the seat with Shaker tape and finish the chair. It was not Shaker perfect but that no longer mattered to me; it was simply a gift I wanted to give to Eliza. I brought it to the porch and presented it to her. She looked at it rather tentatively. "Don't worry," I reassured her. "It is for you. Enjoy it!" She sat down and rocked back against the white-clapboard side of the house. The chair's finials hit the wall and there went the finish. As it happened, this didn't matter to either of us. She enjoyed the gift and I was delighted in the giving. The chair to this day sits in our living room as a reminder of what can happen when we are tempted under the form of a greater good to an exaggeration of generosity.

———

Mother Teresa of Calcutta was once asked what she thought the real value of her efforts among India's poor might be, given that she was able to serve so few when the needs were so great. She responded that her work was to attend to each person as a child of God without being overwhelmed. The vastness of the poverty she encountered did not stop her and her sisters from doing all they were able to do. As she explained: "We ourselves feel that what we are doing is just a drop in the ocean. But, the ocean would be less because of that missing drop."

———

In the last book of the Bible, the Revelation to John, the writer describes Satan as "the accuser of our comrades." If you are like me, you have within you an interior accusing voice that says things like, "That's not good enough . . . You really messed up . . . There you go again . . . How could you have forgotten . . . " This voice can immobilize me in a state of self-castigation.

The word "Satan" in Hebrew means "adversary." Satan, as adversary, may be thought of as a false conscience inciting us to self-directed hostility and judgment. As such, he can appear as an angel of light because, of course, shouldn't we be aware of our failings? Yes, we should, but the deeper truth is that God's mercy and compassion overrule our fixation on our "dust and sin," to echo the words of George Herbert. As Father Herbert McCabe O.P. wisely observed: "God forgives us, not to make us acceptable to him, but to make him more acceptable to us."

⎯⎯⎯⎯⎯

Do not be conformed to this world, but be transformed by the renewing of your minds, so that you may discern what is the will of God—what is good and acceptable and perfect. —Romans 12:2

One of my wisest teachers of the art of discernment and the making of choices has been Ignatius Loyola (1491–1556), the founder of the Society of Jesus. I return again and again to Ignatius's *Spiritual Exercises* and *The Meditation on the Two Standards* to try to sort out for myself what is going on in my life and my reactions to it. The acuity of his spiritual and psychological insights is a true gift to me in the most ordinary of daily events and decisions.

At their heart, the *Spiritual Exercises* are a structured pathway leading to self-awareness and spiritual freedom that enables those making the exercises to be one with the risen Christ in companionship and service to the needy world. Appended to the *Spiritual Exercises* are Ignatius's *Rules for the Discernment of Spirits*. The rules are, in sum, an invitation to an awareness of the positive and negative polarities that move within all of us, which he describes as the "good spirit" and "evil spirit." Our reaction to these spirits largely shapes our perceptions and determines our actions.

Ignatius speaks of "the enemy of human nature" who keeps us unaware of our cyclical or negative ways of seeing or being that we have come to accept as normal. "That's just the way I am," we might say, and leave unquestioned a dimension of our behavior that calls out for scrutiny and possible change. When we are held in thrall to such embedded patterns, Ignatius says the good spirit breaks in and interrupts the pattern through "the sting of remorse." Suddenly we wake up and say: No more! Enough!

The prodigal son in the Gospel of Luke is a case in point. This young man leaves home and family, taking his inheritance with him, and goes out to see the world, so to speak. Then, having "squandered his property in dissolute living," he finds himself reduced to feeding pigs. For a Jewish boy, feeding pigs must have been the lowest form of labor. I have no doubt he was immobilized in a sense of helplessness, self-pity, and shame. Then, one day, we are told, he "came to himself." That is, something broke through his dark feelings and he said, in effect: "Enough! I'll go home and ask my father to take me on as a hired hand because I am no longer worthy to be called his son." We might say it was "the sting of remorse" that broke through the seeming hopelessness of the situation and offered him the possibility of a liberating choice. Such moments of "coming to ourselves" can occur without warning. Suddenly light floods our darkened minds without any apparent cause, or someone calls us to mindfulness or speaks a word of convicting truth. Or, again, a passage in the Bible or some other book, or some life-changing experience, can serve to wake us up to our less-than-life "stuckness."

Ignatius also speaks about times of consolation and desolation: that is, moods that overtake us, much the way dark clouds or sunshine determine the "mood" of the weather. Periods of consolation and desolation occur again and again in the normal unfolding of our lives. It is very easy for us at such times to become victims of forces that take us away from an accurate reading of what God is doing, and how we are being invited to respond.

In times of consolation we feel alive and filled with energy and Paul's words find deep resonance within us: "I can do all things through [Christ] who strengthens me." When we are in a state of consolation we are most vulnerable to the "enemy of human nature" who can lead us into "exaggerations of generosity."

In times of desolation we feel sad and dejected as the negative fills the whole screen of our consciousness, occluding anything positive and landing us in the "slough of despond," as John Bunyan has it in his allegory *The Pilgrim's Progress*. We feel isolated, unappreciated, self-pitying, and are particularly prone to seeking solace in some comforting and self-indulgent behavior, such as over-eating, drinking to excess, binge-watching television, or something more destructive. We can be overcome by a sense of inevitability, as though we had no choice and, as a result, fall deeper and deeper into a state of hopelessness.

Ignatius offers a caution: in times of desolation do not change a decision you made earlier in a time of consolation. For example, let's say you look at peeling paint in your kitchen and decide a fresh coat is needed. Sounds good. Then, a difficult conversation with a co-worker throws you into desolation. And, the kitchen? Well, you are obviously too inept, you say, to paint it yourself, and you could not possibly afford to have a professional do it, and who really cares about the peeling paint anyway? It's good enough for you . . . This, Ignatius would say, is not the way to go. Rather, he would urge you to trace the path of the desolation back to where it began. Think back to that conversation with the co-worker and what effect it had. In so doing the negativity that has taken center stage in your consciousness may be reduced in size and no longer fill the whole frame. We are wise to be aware of the disproportionate emotional power of the negative.

While I was the Bishop of Chicago, a priest came to see me one day and told me in dejected tones that he thought he should resign because his parish was opposed to him and his ministry. I reminded him that when he first arrived at the parish he felt he and the congregation had been perfectly matched by the Holy Spirit. "Now they are all against me," was his reply. As we talked it became clear that the "all" was two persons in the parish, and his great offense had been to move the lectern without consultation. The very act of having to recount the particulars from beginning to end, and share it with another person, reframed them in such a way that, realizing how the negative had overwhelmed reality, he rather sheepishly said, "I guess I had better not resign." Unsurprisingly, I agreed.

Ignatius bids us to act against the desolation through "much prayer." Though this is often very effective, there are times when "much prayer" seems to focus me on my negative feelings and land me even deeper in my state of desolation. Acting against the desolation can also take the form of doing something concrete that takes me out of myself and is contrary to the mood that has overtaken me. Something as simple as writing an email, making a telephone call, or raking leaves can counteract the forces of the negative. Such action may require a concerted effort because desolation can provide its own dark comfort and tempt us to wallow in feelings of sadness and self-pity.

I once knew a nun, well-seasoned in the ways of the Spirit, who, when overcome by desolation, would repair to the fur salon in a nearby department store and swirl about in a mink coat in front of a three-way mirror. She told me it always worked and, thus liberated, she would return to her ministry with new energy.

———————

The Meditation on the Two Standards can be extremely helpful in discernment as we read the scripture of our lives. The two standards are two battle flags. Ignatius had been a soldier and uses a great deal of military imagery in the *Spiritual Exercises.* In this meditation he invites us to imagine two armies: one standing under the battle flag of Satan and the other under the battle flag of Christ. If you stand under the battle flag of Satan, you will find yourself caught up in a dynamic of riches, leading to honor, leading to pride. Riches here means our tendency to want to possess things. Honor means how we understand ourselves and define ourselves in relation to our possessions. Pride then becomes the private world we construct around ourselves to protect our sense of self, based on what we possess.

Riches can take many forms. One's profession can become one's riches: in my case it is ordained ministry. I can define who I am and derive my self-worth from the fact that I am ordained. The context in which I exercise my ministry can become my world. For ministry one can substitute any number of professions and obtain the same dynamic. We become what we do and our worth is derived from the acknowledgment and approbation we receive from others.

Riches can also take less obvious forms. Anger, for example, can become a form of riches. For some, hostility is a primary motivating force. Their anger becomes a precious possession by which they define themselves and from which they draw strength. To relinquish their anger would be to lose their identity. The daily news is replete with examples of this form of riches, both on a personal and a global level.

Low self-worth can be another subtle form of riches. If we cling to a sense of being unable to meet the demands of life, we can be passive and excuse ourselves from responsibility, all the while deluding ourselves that we are virtuous and humble.

The battle flag of Christ represents a very different dynamic, which Ignatius describes in terms of poverty, contempt, and humility—the opposite of riches, honor, and pride. In this context, poverty means the ability to recognize everything as a gift from God rather than as a personal possession. When we are standing under the battle flag of Christ we know that the talents and competencies we possess to do our work in the world, whatever that may be, are not our possession but rather a gift we have been given.

Contempt does not mean we are seeking to be treated with contempt, but rather that we are willing to endure hostility or rejection for the sake of truth. We are eager to use our gifts in ways that God intends, and to be freed from needing others to think well of us. This was true of Jesus and many of the prophets, up to our own day. Their sense of being agents of God's larger purposes gave them the ability to risk speaking and doing the truth even when it exposed them to ridicule and hatred.

While pride is to be closed in on oneself and to create, as it were, a private world in which to protect one's riches and honor, humility is a stance of openness and availability.

In this meditation Ignatius invites us to examine our lives and ask ourselves where we stand in relation to these two flags. In some areas of our lives we could be standing under the battle flag of Satan and in other areas we might be standing under the battle flag of Christ. The two flags, and the dynamics associated with each, help us to explore our patterns of thinking and behaving and thus gain insight into our interior disposition. They help us to see if we are closed in upon ourselves or open to whatever form God's larger purposes might take.

I have learned this about myself: my reaction to criticism can be a clue to which battle flag I am standing under. I am embarrassed to remember that many years ago when I was newly ordained I was honored to give a retreat to a very sophisticated and spiritually mature group of men and women who had a strong devotion to St. Francis of Assisi. As a tour de force, I concluded the retreat with an elaborate and, in my view, brilliant exposition of Francis's hymn of creation, "The Canticle of the Sun." After the retreat I read the attendees' evaluations. They were filled with appreciation and gratitude for the depth of what I had offered. As I read them I mouthed the words of the old prayer: "to God be the glory." Then, suddenly I came across a comment that the retreat had been "fine" until we came to the exposition of Francis's hymn, at which point "it all fell apart." I was stung and offended. I tried to imagine who had written this. I saw particular faces in my mind's eye and decided that whoever the person was, they certainly were not up to receiving the acuity of my insights. This one negative response managed to overrule all the favorable comments, and I descended into a place of desolation. Then, invoking the advice of St. Ignatius, I managed to stand back and take stock of the situation. It didn't take me long to realize I was standing under the battle flag of Satan and had become the victim of riches, honor, and pride. My "brilliant insights" had become my riches rather than a gift to offer. The walls of my pride had been breached, and my honor—my self-approval—had been threatened. With gratitude for the insight, I prayed: *Lord, make me an instrument, not on my terms, but on yours.*

Some years later during my years as the Bishop of Chicago, much to my surprise, I found myself able to stand in a very difficult place of truth and endure with equanimity the corporate rage of several hundred people because of a decision I had made. Their much-loved rector had left to take another position and the congregation was outraged when I did not comply with their request that his young assistant take his place. With some degree of trepidation, I entered the parish hall. The atmosphere was tense and frostily hostile. After I explained the reasons behind my decision, a woman rose to her feet and declared that she had analyzed my handwriting. "Your handwriting, Bishop, reveals a keen mind but *no* heart!" As she sat down, the crowd roared an enthusiastic Amen. Curiously, I felt no ill will toward them, even in this display. I knew my decision was the right one, though it was impossible for the congregation at that point in their life to understand or welcome it. Some months later one of the parish leaders who had been among the angriest at the meeting told me, somewhat apologetically, that my decision had indeed been right, and thanked me for sticking to it. Reflecting on that experience afterwards, I was grateful I had been enabled to stand calmly in a place of truth and accept with a peaceful spirit the opprobrium that was cast upon me. I had been standing under the battle flag of Christ.

———

"Teach me discernment and knowledge," prays the psalmist. I do not think this prayer is an appeal for a body of information or an instruction booklet. Rather, it gives voice to the desire to be rooted in the deep mystery of God from whom we draw our life, and through whom we discover who we are and are called to be. As we make choices along life's way, discernment and awareness attune us to the motions of the Spirit, liberating us from what is false and constricting. And, as St. Paul tell us: "where the Spirit of the Lord is, there is freedom."

Acquiring a Heart:
The Complexity
of Being Fully Human

Persons in the Making

We are all persons in the making
and in a real sense we are
making and re-making one another.
But how often personal relationships
are marred by hasty, partial or
over-severe judgments.
We must help one another,
not judge one another,
and we must leave the final judgment
to the Divine Patience.
One of the greatest promises
in the New Testament is that
we are accepted in the Beloved.
Let us try to be the ministers
of acceptance.
                                    —Eric Symes Abbott,
                        Dean of Westminster, 1959–1974

It has been a custom for Phoebe and me to read a book aloud together during our summer vacation. One summer I suggested a book rather provocatively titled *Marriage: Dead or Alive*. The author, Adolf Guggenbühl-Craig, a Jungian psychiatrist, makes the point that marriage is not just for the happiness of the spouses, but for their salvation: that is, their becoming who they are most truly called to be through the give and take of their relationship. As Phoebe and I read the book together, what we already knew at some level became more plain. That is: we, in all our relationships and interactions, form and shape one another—for good or ill, be it within the context of a marriage, family, school, work, or some other form of community. The free-standing individual, which is so much a part of American mythology, is an aberration because relationship in community is integral to our being fully human and fully alive.

I am struck by St. Paul's insistence in the Letter to the Ephesians that our maturity in Christ is not an individual accomplishment but something we achieve together. I am also mindful that the prayer Jesus teaches his followers is the prayer of a community. It begins not "My Father," but "Our Father."

An inclination toward community is a fundamental human instinct. We can be taken out of our private worlds into an expression of community in many ways: a ball game, a disaster, a civic event, an experience of common worship, even an exercise class—and suddenly we find our world enlarged as we become part of something that transcends as well as includes us.

Sometimes community catches us quite by surprise and in serendipitous ways. I remember once having dinner with friends in a crowded restaurant when suddenly a young man at a nearby table leapt to his feet and cried out: "She said yes!" All conversation stopped, all heads turned, and then everyone in the restaurant burst into cheers and applause. His new fiancée blushed and beamed. In that instant, we all became one in our shared joy for the young couple. Very moved by the moment, I sent them a bottle of champagne!

———

Before I was invited to be the rector of St. Andrew's in Yardley, Pennsylvania, I was interviewed by a small group of parish leaders. Among them was one woman to whom others always deferred. Miss Gladys Harper was undoubtedly the matriarch of the parish, a status undergirded by the fact that earlier generations of her family had supplied the funds to build the parish house. She was the secretary of the Pennsylvania Women's

Christian Temperance Union, and a formidable presence in the community. After listening with some degree of patience to my responses to questions from other members of the group Miss Harper piped up: "Father Griswold, what would you do if the young people of the parish chose not to attend a meeting with a visiting missionary and went off instead to a dance?" I felt sure the dance would be more fun for them than the missionary, and said as much. Miss Harper smiled grimly and said nothing. Much later I learned that after I left she had declared firmly, "If that young man comes to the parish, I am leaving."

I came, and Miss Harper remained, and continued as head of the parish chapter of the Daughters of the King, an Anglican order devoted to prayer and evangelism. In my first days at St. Andrew's they invited me to meet with them: a group of ancient women, or so it seemed to me at the time. I innocently asked what their purpose might be. Miss Harper, not missing a beat, replied: "We are the *handmaidens* of the rector." This was the first word to me, and an unsettling one it was, that I was to have handmaidens. As it happened, over the years Miss Harper and I became fast friends. At her invitation, I once served as chaplain to the state gathering of the WCTU and celebrated the Eucharist, using grape juice instead of wine, of course.

As we are all interconnected—limbs and members of Christ's body—it is not surprising that we bump up against one another and, in ways that surprise us and contradict our previously held opinions, are thus changed.

A new heart I will give you, and a new spirit I will put within you; and I will remove from your body the heart of stone and give you a heart of flesh. —Ezekiel 36:26

The heart, in the Judeo-Christian tradition, is understood not simply as the seat of our emotions, but as the dwelling place of God's Spirit: the agent and minister of God's love. It is the Spirit's task, in collaboration with our own spirit, to transform and liberate our hearts of stone—that is hearts that are impermeable to the movements and motions of God's love—into hearts of flesh able to receive and share what God so eagerly desires to foster and mature within us.

The human heart has a special prominence both in scripture and in the early tradition of the church. "Acquire a heart and you shall be saved," is another saying that comes to us from the desert tradition. It refers to our hearts being transformed and made merciful, which happens not primarily through our own efforts, but through the Spirit of Christ finding a home within us, often aided by our encounters with the Miss Harpers we meet along the way.

Aware or unaware as we may be, the Spirit is always close at hand, frequently under the cover of seemingly random encounters and events that appear to be utterly inconsequential. Yet, all the while, without our knowing, we are being changed and our hearts are being rendered merciful. Divine mystery encounters us in every moment, clothed in the events that constitute our personal history and the stuff of our days.

———————

Religious language is not needed to describe ways in which we, in the words of Eric Abbott, are "all persons in the making and in a real sense we are making and re-making one another." Because I speak from the experience of my own life, I use Christian terms to describe this lifelong process of shaping and being shaped by life from birth to death. Others, from their experiences, will name their own truths in their own vocabularies. The classical vocabulary of Christianity helps me to be present and responsive, and indeed curious and wondering, in the face of life's mystery. It invites me to attend to the intimations of the Divine clothed in our everyday experiences: the choices, relationships, joys, and sorrows that constitute our daily round. Looking through the lens of faith does not protect me from life's vagaries and vicissitudes. Rather, it gives me the desire and courage to read the scripture of my life, as best I can, with unblinded sight.

———————

Many centuries ago St. Isaac of Syria was asked what defined a merciful heart; he replied:

It is a heart that burns with love for the whole of creation—for humanity, for the birds, for the beasts, for the demons, for every creature. When those with hearts such as this think of the creatures or look at them, their eyes are filled with tears. An overwhelming compassion makes their hearts grow small and weak, and they cannot endure to hear or see any suffering, even the smallest pain, inflicted upon any creature. Therefore they never cease to pray, with tears even for the irrational animals, for the enemies of truth, and for those who do them evil, asking that they may be guarded and receive God's mercy. And for the reptiles also they pray with a great compassion which rises up endlessly in their hearts until they shine again and are glorious like God.

The merciful heart St. Isaac describes is the fruit of our availability to the Source that lies at the center of the Universe, which some of us name as God and Christians see revealed in the person of Jesus of Nazareth. The acquisition of a merciful heart, therefore, is beyond our imagination or psychological effort. It involves our encounter with God's own mercy, which is woven into the fabric of our being in creation but can be obscured and compromised by our life in the world.

———

Beloved, let us love one another, because love is from God
. . . Whoever does not love does not know God, for God
is love.   —1 John 4:7

Love as an abstraction is one thing, but love experienced concretely, in a relationship with another human being, as Dorothy Day used to say, quoting Dostoyevsky, "is a harsh and dreadful thing." Love can be costly, and demanding. Love can be painful, and purifying as well—rubbing off sharp edges. Love can also heal and restore.

Contrary to common perceptions, to love, to be *in* love, is not simply to *feel* something. Of course, we do *feel* something, many things, sometimes conflicting things. However, love goes beyond our feelings. Love is not incidental, or optional, today and yesterday, and perhaps tomorrow, if we are fortunate. Our being able to love, giving ourselves over to love, is the work of God in us. To love is to see as God sees, or at least to want to see one another as God sees each of us, as beloved and "precious in God's sight."

It is difficult to give what you have never received. When a child grows up in a context where the energy of love is absent, their ability to love may be severely compromised. Such children are not practiced in the mutual receiving and giving of love. Here I am reminded that Jesus says to his disciples: *As I am loved by the Father so have I loved you. Abide in my love.* Jesus can only share with his disciples the love he himself has received from the Father: *Abba.* And, in commanding his disciples to love, Jesus is saying: *love out of the love with which I have loved you. Give to others the gift I have given you.*

Called into Companionship with Christ

The person of Jesus Christ, the "Anointed One" or "the Messiah" as the name can be variously translated, is not simply an historical figure worthy of emulation. Christ is the archetype of fully developed personhood. The glory of God, declares St. Irenaeus, is the human person fully alive, and it is through our companionship with Christ that we become fully human and fully alive. St. Augustine says we are a mystery even to our own selves. God alone has full knowledge of our personal mystery. God alone knows who we, in grace and truth, are called to be.

"If anyone is in Christ there is a new creation . . . The life I now live is now not my own but the life Christ lives in me . . . For freedom Christ has set us free . . ." The freedom St. Paul describes here is the freedom to come to maturity and fullness of selfhood through intimate union and companionship with Christ. However, companionship with Christ is not about imagining an ideal self and then asking God to bring it into

being. Nor does it mean the removal of all the idiosyncrasies—
the limitations and imperfections—that make us uniquely who
we are. Rather, companionship with Christ means allowing
Christ's Spirit to blow where it wills in the depths of our being,
fashioning and refashioning us, not according to our own
desires, but in accordance with God's loving desire for us—a
desire that exceeds all we might ask or imagine. The fruit of
our companionship with Christ is to find ourselves open and
available to the world around us such that Christ can be present
in and through the particularity of our own lives.

In the early 1960s while I was a curate at the Church of the
Redeemer I led a discussion group for young women from
nearby Bryn Mawr College. During one of our sessions a student
raised a question that surprised me: "Can women be ordained
to the priesthood?" I replied with a dismissive laugh: "Certainly
not!" At that point in the life of the church the question had
not been broadly raised, and I felt no need to explain further.
To my mind, the Catholic tradition which had shaped me, and
which I saw as faithfully adhered to by Anglicanism, precluded
such a possibility. Several years later the Episcopal Church
began to discuss the possibility of women's ordination and I
was conflicted. Part of me could see the reasonableness and
rightness of such a possibility. The other part of me felt this
would threaten its Catholic heritage.

Time went on and the discussion within the church continued.
Then, a few years later when I had become the rector of St.
Andrew's, a young woman I had recently baptized and presented
for confirmation came to see me and told me she would like to
enroll in a theological seminary but she did not know if she was
called to be ordained. She went off to seminary and a year later
returned and told me she believed she was called to be a priest.
She was so articulate and clear about her sense of call that my
reservations fell away. When an abstract theological question
became embodied in the life of a person I trusted and respected,
my view was changed. Her journey became my journey as well,
and my limited understanding of God's ways was expanded to

embrace something new. Through such encounters, our hearts can indeed be transformed from stone to flesh.

The young woman was Geralyn Wolf, who was subsequently ordained deacon and priest, and later elected and ordained as the Bishop of Rhode Island. Surely it is a sign of the divine sense of humor that I, who originally had questions about the rightness of it all, had the privilege of being the preacher at all three of her ordinations.

———————

There are varieties of gifts, but the same Spirit.
—1 Corinthians 12:4

By the early 1970s the interdenominational charismatic renewal movement had found its way into the life of the Episcopal Church. The word "charismatic" is derived from the Greek word meaning "gifts" or "grace," and the movement sought to renew the life of the church by re-appropriating the gifts of the Holy Spirit poured out upon the early church on the day of Pentecost. Among those gifts was the gift of tongues, that is, the ability to speak a kind of spiritual language, which St. Paul mentions as one of the gifts of the Spirit.

Around that time I came across a book that described steps one might take to be given this gift. Though somewhat unsure, but open to the possibility, I went into St. Andrew's, knelt in front of the altar, and followed the prescribed steps. It was a still and cloudless summer day. Suddenly out of nowhere a strong wind rose, engulfing the church. Then, just as suddenly as it had risen, it ceased, and I heard, as it were, a voice within saying: "Frank, this gift is not meant for you." Strangely, I felt no disappointment but rather consolation. I had made myself available as best I could to God's Spirit, and that was all that mattered.

Years later, during my days as the Bishop of Chicago, a priest appeared in my office one day with what she described as a mandate from the Lord. "I am here today," she said, "to give you the gift of tongues. Kneel down!" I was taken aback and caught by surprise. Something within me wanted to say, "this gift is not meant for me," but then I thought that perhaps she really had come, sent by the Lord, and I might be resisting the Spirit. I knelt down and she prayed over me for some time. Then, pausing and looking down, she said, "open your mouth and let it flow." In desperation I emitted a jumble of sounds but I knew in my heart they were self-induced and not the work of the Holy Spirit. Soon after she left, having accomplished her task. Though I felt appreciative of her efforts, I was greatly relieved that the session had ended. As St. Paul reminds us, there are varieties of gifts allotted to us in different ways, just as the Spirit chooses. That is, we don't all have the gift of tongues.

Embracing the Paschal Mystery

We thank you, Father, for the water of Baptism. In it we are buried with Christ in his death. By it we share in his resurrection. Through it we are reborn by the Holy Spirit.
                     —The Book of Common Prayer

Some years ago I ran across these startling words from Flannery O'Connor: "We are crucified by the church." At first I was shocked, but as I thought about it and reflected on my own experiences I realized that no human institution or context is immune to the paschal pattern of death and resurrection: a pattern that meets us wherever we are intensely present and engaged, and in the midst of the most intimate and ordinary, and sometimes altogether ridiculous, occasions of our lives.

The *paschal*, or *Easter*, mystery is a term used to describe the unity of Jesus's death and resurrection as one event, not simply in the past but as a dynamic pattern that reproduces itself in our lives. Our lives reveal to us the paradox that Jesus himself sets before us: losing becomes the way to finding, and by dying to ourselves we find something within us has been enlarged rather than diminished. This can be an attitude, a sense of self, an understanding of others, and thus the way is opened to what Jesus describes as "abundant life." Given that through baptism we are "buried with Christ," it should not surprise us that we live within the costly reality of this paschal pattern.

Death and resurrection accost us again and again as our lives unfold. Dying and rising is more than a religious construct; it is a fundamental law of existence which is certainly writ large in the natural world. And, indeed, those of us who are called to preach the gospel might ask ourselves how we can authentically proclaim something we have not actually lived. A friend once described to me the baptism of an infant at her parish. As the water was poured on the baby's head the newly baptized let out a piercing shriek, much to the embarrassment of her parents and godparents. Without skipping a beat, the priest said to the congregation: "You'd be crying too if you had just been buried with Christ!" This was much more than a humorous aside. His words carried with them the conviction of one for whom they were real.

Where we most truly live is where we meet the paschal mystery. In my case, I have known it intimately within the life of the church, as I have experienced for myself the truth of Flannery O'Connor's words. Fidelity to Christ has required me again and again to relinquish my ways of seeing and understanding the church. My sense of what was unchangeable, my secure rock, has undergone drastic alteration and required me to let go of what I thought were unchanging truths, both about the institution and about myself in relation to it.

As well I have lived the reality of the paschal mystery through experiences of unwarranted criticism or the misunderstanding of my words or actions, through suspicion of my motives, through the anger and disappointment of others because of my failure to fulfill their expectations. In such ways the opprobrium that attached itself to Jesus can attach itself to us and, in my experience, can most certainly attach itself to pastors. In such circumstances, feelings of resentment, self-pity, anger, and revenge are not foreign to us, nor is the practice of nursing our wounds and playing out in our minds retorts to those who offend us, or giving free rein to the seductive deliciousness of self-pity.

I well understand these feelings because I am subject to them.

I take great comfort in the fact that the writer of the Letter to the Hebrews tells us that Jesus was in every way tempted as we are. This suggests to me that no feeling or emotion that courses through the human spirit is alien to the One who took upon himself the full weight and reality of our humanity.

Being crucified by the church is most certainly present in the life of a bishop. As I have observed, it is ironic that the more grandiose our forms of address the more we are interiorly stripped and obliged to face the cross. I have often thought that the purple shirts worn by many bishops as a sign of their office are the perfect setup for us to become targets of other people's angers and discontents.

We live in a culture of upward mobility. Success is cast in terms of bigger, better, and the measures of wealth. Climbing up the ladder is the common expectation in most professional arenas, including the church. Contrary to this, St. Benedict in his *Rule for Monks* talks about climbing the ladder of humility by going down it. He describes a counter direction that leads not necessarily to what is bigger and better in this world's terms, but deeper and truer in terms of who we are and are called to be by God.

"In order to possess what you do not possess, you must go by way of dispossession," observes T.S. Eliot, echoing St. John of the Cross. This paradox lies at the heart of the paschal mystery, and it only makes sense to those who, in union with Christ, dare to embrace it in all its stark reality. And yet, what is revealed is not death and diminishment, but life—not life as we formerly knew it, but as the One who is our life reveals it.

The heart of your word is truth. —Psalm 119:160

During my years in Chicago I met David Tracy, a highly regarded Roman Catholic theologian who taught at the University of Chicago Divinity School. Our meeting led me to his theological writings, and I was particularly engaged by what he calls the "pluriformity of truth," namely that truth is multidimensional. This means, as Fidel Castro observed, that truth is invariably larger than any one person's perspective.

I also came across an observation made by the Greek Orthodox theologian, John Zizioulas, namely that "truth is discovered in communion." That is, truth of its nature is dialogical and involves a willingness to engage together in a common search. The combination of these two approaches made me realize that my grasp of truth is limited by my life experience and view of the world, my culture, my education, and my internal disposition. And, the same is true for all of us. The only way I can enlarge my truth is by being exposed and open to the dimensions of truth expressed in the experiences and understandings of others.

It is worth noting that the words "conversation" and "conversion" come from the same Latin root, meaning "to turn" or "to change." Conversation has an enormous power to lead to conversion, particularly when we risk opening ourselves to one another in trust and with undefended hearts. True conversation is a spiritual discipline whereby we render ourselves vulnerable to being changed in some way by the truth present in another. Conversation is not about the triumph of one point of view over another but about the discovery amidst our differences of a common ground of mutual respect, and even affection, where we can stand together.

It is better to begin such a conversation with what we share rather than with our points of disagreement. If we begin with where we disagree we tend to be defensive rather than receptive. For example, when confronted by divergent opinions among Christians, if we begin together by addressing a common question, such as "who is Jesus for you?" we open the way for mutual exploration and the possibility of establishing points of common understanding before we engage our differences. Such a disciplined approach to conversation is in no way limited to the spiritual or religious realm but is equally valuable for dealing with controversial issues in the political arena—from the neighborhood to the international level.

While serving as Presiding Bishop I participated in the annual meetings of the primates, that is the bishops who head the thirty-nine provinces of the Anglican Communion. Each day after breakfast we gathered in small groups of six to eight to reflect together on a passage of scripture. The scripture gave us a common starting point that drew us together, even while revealing marked differences in interpretation and application. We looked through the lens of the gospel at the very different circumstances in which we lived and were called to minister. As we considered some of the struggles Jesus faced in his life we were led, with increasing trust, to share the difficulties we each faced in our own contexts. This emboldened a brother primate at one of our morning sessions to ask me what he feared would sound like a "stupid" or "incredibly naive" question. "When a couple is two men, does one of them wear a dress?" I was stunned. I realized his was a genuine question that indicated how different our experiences and cultures were. I told him no, and explained that if he met a male couple they would both be dressed in men's clothes. He thanked me, genuinely grateful. I felt great affection for my brother who dared to ask such a question. He was able to ask his question, and I was able to answer it with respect, because of the trust that had been established over the preceding days.

As our time together ended, another primate who came from a culture very different from my own exclaimed: "You know, the Holy Spirit can do different things in different places!" At that point we looked at one another with delight and surprise and said, "Of course." Along the way we had been converted to a grateful awareness of how much we shared as true brothers in Christ. Conversion had occurred not at the level of the mind but in the depths of our hearts. Though our different points of view remained largely intact, our relationships had been greatly altered and the perspectives we each held when we entered the conversation had been enlarged and expanded.

In discussions with people from other parts of the world I came to realize how problematic it is to assume that you and someone from a different culture, speaking another language, understand each other. In some sense, translation always involves paraphrase. For example, at another meeting of the primates, I discovered that words I might use as a neutral descriptor such as "homosexuality" ("gay" was too complicated to explain) when translated into another language became the words used to describe a violent sex act, and therefore it sounded as if I condoned sexual violence.

In accepting the premise that we are for one another—for one another's salvation—which I do, we are led into the complexities of human relationships: the delights, the messiness, the awkwardness. All of this is part of being alive in the world. The very angularities and unsettling points of view of another may be exactly the way in which the Spirit of truth is seeking to deepen and broaden our personal experience of truth. My firmly held truth may stand in need of the expansion that occurs only when I make space for the truth embodied in another.

We are always learning more: about the world, the workings of the human body, the cosmos. Old truth is expanded, and sometimes corrected, by new truth. This is not only the case in the realm of science; it is also true as we are able to make room in ourselves for God's ever-unfolding mystery.

In the Gospel of John, Jesus declares: *"I still have many things to say to you but you cannot bear them now. When the Spirit of truth comes, he will guide you into all the truth . . . he will take what is mine and reveal it to you."* So, we might say here that the Spirit reveals truth only as we are able to receive it.

Humankind, as T.S. Eliot tells us, "cannot bear very much reality." The same can be said of truth—and what is reality other than truth? God's compassion is such that we are not overburdened with more than we are able to bear. And, the Spirit of truth, who knows us better than we know ourselves, often works by stealth and indirection.

Truth also has a relational dimension. Jesus does not say I will *tell* you the truth. He says I *am* the truth. There exists, therefore, an interior dimension of truth we gain through companionship with Christ, who meets us as the Spirit of truth in the intimate and personal depths of our being.

In this regard, certitude can be the enemy of truth because once we have set limits to what we understand as truth we are impermeable to any new, and possibly unsettling, information. Over the years I have had to confront my own certitude: those limits I set to protect myself from a truth that could require alteration in my perceptions of myself, of the world, and of God's mysterious ways.

~

For my thoughts are not your thoughts, nor are your ways
my ways, says the Lord.   —Isaiah 55:8

The word "orthodox" is sometimes used in church circles as a weapon. Saying that someone is "unorthodox" brands them as being out of touch with the Truth. In fact, the term itself does not mean right belief, though it is frequently used as if it did, but rather "right praise." Thus, orthodoxy is, first, about worship rather than carefully reasoned theological opinion. And, to praise or pray "rightly" is to open oneself to the full truth and authenticity of God's mystery as it undergirds life in all its forms. The church is always seeking to praise and pray "rightly" in order to expand its availability to the ways of God. God's ways in their ever-unfolding fullness exceed our present and limited understanding or comprehension.

As the church in its early centuries sought to describe its experience of God's mystery, it found it had to make room for something else: namely, paradox. That is, God's ways are not linear. At times they can seem "crooked," and can even hold together things that appear contradictory. We tend to think in terms of *either/or* while paradox is a matter of *both/and*: two seemingly irreconcilable realities are held together in tension, and that tension itself is a manifestation of truth.

One of the most dramatic instances of thinking paradoxically in the life of the church has to do with the person of Jesus Christ. In the year 451, bishops gathered at the Council of Chalcedon with a difficult task before them: to come to a common understanding of the nature of Christ. They were not of one mind, and the theological climate of the time out of which they came led to various views being couched in either/or terms: Christ was *either* human, *or* Christ was divine. Some said he was fully divine and only appeared to be human. Others held that he was fully human and only appeared to be divine. In the end the bishops came to what is known as the Chalcedonian Definition, which states that Christ is both fully human *and* fully divine. And there it is: two seemingly irreconcilable natures—humanity and divinity—held together in one person.

Paradox is shown again in the doctrine of the Trinity, namely that God is one and at the same time manifested as *three* persons: Father, Son, and Holy Spirit. Gregory of Nazianzus, a fourth-century theologian, was not shy in declaring that, with respect to the classical definition of the Trinity, "both the distinction and the union alike are paradoxical."

Though many of us like things to be black or white, right or wrong, and sometimes find it difficult to live within the tension of paradoxical situations, we manage to do so every day, particularly in our relationships. People close to us often manifest attitudes, traits, and ways of being that run counter to our sense of "how things ought to be." And yet, we are able to make room for, and live with, the tension of both the perceived ideal and what actually is. Love makes it possible to live with paradox.

Through baptism we are bound together in solidarities not of our own choosing.   —Rowan Williams, Archbishop of Canterbury (2002–12)

My baptism on that long-ago January day, as was common in those times, was a private occasion in the presence of friends and family. This is no longer the usual practice. The Prayer Book of the Episcopal Church calls for Baptism to be celebrated "within the Eucharist as the chief service on a Sunday or other feast." This is theologically appropriate, given that our growth in Christ and our coming "to maturity, to the measure of the full stature of Christ" (Ephesians 4:13), involves life with others, and indeed, some of them may well not be "of our own choosing." In fact, their presence as brothers and sisters in Christ may challenge and disconcert us.

In his description of the church as the body of Christ, St. Paul declares that the wholeness of the body depends on the relationship of its multiple limbs and organs. Each limb has its own unique function that contributes to the life of the whole body. Each of us, Paul tells us, has been given some gift or manifestation of Christ's fullness, which together contributes to the building up of the body. In baptism, through the action of the Holy Spirit, Christ draws us to himself and takes us out of our presumed separateness into a new web of relationships that unites us with others. Questions of personal affinity, of whether we like someone or not, whether we agree or not, are not the point. Something far more fundamental has happened: God has knit us together in a body not of our own making, and Christ is the head and consciousness of this body. What more dynamic, or intimate, or essential relationship can there be than that of growing together through the gifts of one another into the fullness of who we have been created to be?

Paul also declares that "the eye cannot say to the hand I have no need of you." He says that if all body parts were the same the body would cease to exist. Therefore, difference and distinction and the tensions that often accompany them are integral to the body's health and wholeness. The church in Paul's day had its share of differing points of view and divisive issues, especially as the church expanded beyond Judaism to include Gentile converts. Paul's vision had immediate application and relevance to what was occurring in the life of the infant community. Over the years the notion of the church as the body of Christ has become ever more real to me. It has stood me in good stead and provided the theological ground for the ministry of care and oversight I was called upon to exercise as a bishop.

The polarizing effect of conflicts in our churches reveals that many people on all sides of contentious questions have little sense of what it means to be "church." For them, Paul's notion that Baptism binds us together is simply not a fundamental and shared perception. For many, "church" is determined by those of like mind, while those with contrary points of view are considered suspect or "unfaithful."

Struggle and conflict can properly be a part of living into

God's right ordering of the world and our relationships within it. However, in the midst of the struggles we are often impeded by the various languages we speak that carry with them a whole range of assumptions. There is the language of holiness, which is used in large measure by those of more traditional points of view, and the language of justice, which is more easily spoken by those who consider themselves progressive or liberal. Suspicion and hostility make it difficult for us to hear one another as our vocabularies become mutually exclusive: sin and the cross; new life and resurrection; Jesus as Lord and Savior; Christ as liberator and herald of new creation. Rather than complementing one another, these different ways of naming the vastness of God and God's ways can be seen as alien to one another.

Conversation with a Buddhist Nun

What might we say about God's relation to those who are not baptized? According to scripture, all humankind has been created in the image and likeness of God. For me this means that all of humanity is enfolded and sustained by God's mercy and love and no human being lies outside the boundaries of God's care and concern. All are included in God's embrace— baptized or not, Christian or not, believers or non-believers— whether they acknowledge it fully or don't have the faintest glimmer of it.

The question of God's relation to those who are not baptized became very real to me some years ago while I was visiting the Anglican Church of Korea, where I had been invited to teach and lecture. For six weeks Phoebe and I lived in a small apartment in an Anglican convent set in a walled garden sheltered from the bustle of Seoul. One afternoon one of the nuns invited me to meet with a group of some twenty or so Anglican, Roman Catholic, and Buddhist nuns who have gathered regularly for many years to meditate and pray in silence together for world peace. I was asked to speak about the American monk and spiritual writer Thomas Merton. They were particularly interested in him because his encounter with divine mystery—variously named and understood—had not been confined to Christianity, and they were eager to know more about him.

After the meeting, one of the Buddhist nuns approached me and asked very directly if I, as a Christian, felt obliged to try to convert her to Christianity. I replied with an emphatic "no." I explained that my Christian faith makes me eager to learn how the Divine or Ultimate, known to me as Christ, might be expressing itself in her Buddhist faith and spiritual practice. I went on to tell her that I was eager to discover how truth and spiritual insight conveyed by sacred texts, symbols, and rituals very different from my own might inform, enrich, and enlarge my understanding of how the force I call God is present and active beyond the borders of my Christian faith and experience.

No matter how differently we might describe what we understand as the spiritual realities of life, I believe we are all somehow within one overarching mystery. How very sad it is that our different understandings of this mystery, and our different spiritual practices, which are intended to lead us beyond ourselves and into the depths of the Divine, can instead lead us to erect walls of separation and judgment.

For me as a Christian the true self is discovered in relation to Christ the Word through whom all things have come into being. It is this relationship with Christ, brought about through the Holy Spirit, that constitutes salvation, or one might say, liberation from what is false and constricting in order to become one's true self. Though I have been shaped through a particular religious tradition with its specific forms and practices, along the way these practices have become gateways to an experience of the Divine rather than ends in themselves. In a sense, these forms and practices became the door through which I had to pass. This is a paradox. That is, the specific becomes the entry point to that which is transcendent.

The Children of Abraham

Some years ago, during a visit to Jerusalem, I made an excursion to Hebron to visit the Tomb of the Patriarchs, a vast structure erected by Herod two millennia ago. I did so to fulfill a promise

I had made to my rabbi friend from Chicago, Herman Shalman, who had asked me to pray for him at Abraham's tomb. As I stood before its entrance, I noticed to my left a group of Muslim men gathered around the Quran. And to my right, in the small vestibule set apart as a synagogue, a group of Jewish women were at prayer. As I stood there I thought, here we are, the three children of Abraham, who find it difficult to acknowledge that we are siblings. I found myself wondering why there are three Abrahamic siblings. Perhaps God has revealed dimensions of God's fathomless mystery to three different children to make it clear that not one of them has an exclusive right to God's presence or blessing, and that God's reality transcends any one tradition. Facing Abraham's tomb I imagined myself extending my hands to the right and to the left in solidarity and brotherhood with my Jewish sisters and Muslim brothers. The wideness of God's mercy, which embraces us all, had laid claim to me and expanded my heart.

Returning and Remembering

We shall not cease from exploration, and the end of all our exploring will be to arrive where we started and know the place for the first time.

—T.S. Eliot, "Little Gidding"

Not long ago, on a winter morning, I made my way to the monastery of the Society of Saint John the Evangelist in Cambridge, the place I have come to so often over more than six decades: first as an adolescent, then as a college student, and now as a bishop. During one of the services I looked up at the stained-glass windows that depict founders of religious orders. Across the way St. Ignatius Loyola was looking down at me. After the service I crossed to the other side of the chapel to see who had been above my head. And there he was: Benedict, facing Ignatius. Both had had me in their sights. As I left the chapel I looked up at the window depicting Father Benson, one of the most original theologians in the Anglican tradition. In his founding of his new Society he combined the apostolic

urgency of Ignatius with the communal life and worship so
dominant in Benedict's *Rule for Monks*.

As I stood there in this place I have known so well, I thought
about how, as the seasons of my life have unfolded, Benedict
and Ignatius have been ministers of encouragement and
wisdom, companions, wise teachers in the "school of the Lord's
service," to borrow some words from Benedict's *Rule*. I wonder
now if I had been drawn to these men of the Spirit on my own,
or if they had first drawn me. Perhaps God chose them to be
special guides and friends. Father Benson, too, had become a
friend and guide as his vision of the church as always in a state
of becoming, growing toward the catholicity, the fullness that
alone belongs to God, had become my own.

At that moment, I felt a profound sense of having come home
to where it all started when, at age fifteen, I was sent from St.
Paul's School for spiritual direction. I had been brought back,
full circle to where it had begun, but profoundly changed from
the boy I had been then. All that had happened in this place
flooded back into my mind: the awe I had felt the first time I
came here; my years as an acolyte; the Fathers I had served;
the confessions I had made; the friendships I had known. It
all came together as I experienced the chapel in a new way,
hallowed by all that it now brought to mind. Returning to the
monastery and remembering, I felt both intense gratitude for
all that has been and open to what lay ahead. A verse from
Psalm 108 came to mind: "My heart is firmly fixed, O God, my
heart is fixed . . . "

Knowing as We
Are Known

Now I know only in part;
then I will know fully, even as I have been fully known.
                                        —1 Corinthians 13:12

One evening, in the middle of dinner, a good friend of many years surprised me by asking: "What do you think about heaven?" He is an astute and highly respected theologian, and he asked his question with an intensity that made plain it was personal as well as theological. Though I have preached many funeral sermons, and am very clear that we humans are immortal beings, I have never spent much time thinking about heaven, other than to dismiss notions of harp-playing angels perched on clouds. After a pause to catch my breath I heard myself saying with an intensity that matched his, "Heaven is a dimension of reality we cannot access in our present mode of being. Though it is always at hand, we are limited in our ability to perceive it." I was surprised by the fervor of my response. Clearly, his question had provoked into consciousness something latent within me.

And that is the truth of it. I do believe the life beyond this life is always at hand, and only a thin veil separates this world from what lies ahead for us all. Now and again, in odd and fleeting times-out-of-time, the veil is pulled aside and I become aware of another dimension of reality. In such evanescent moments I sense the presence of those who are no longer in this world. Then, the sensing ends. It eludes me as I try to capture it, and the veil falls once again.

Life when we die, St. Paul tells us, is not taken away but changed: it is transformed by God's love, the same love that drew Jesus through death into resurrection. And what we have known as life—the gathering up of all we have lived from the day of our birth—is then fitted into a larger frame called eternity, which is not a place, but an ever-present dimension of reality that surrounds us and impinges upon us. With a strong conviction of the life that awaits us beyond this life, the early church spoke of one's death day as one's birthday: one's birthday into eternity. We don't so much die out of life as we die into life—life yet to be revealed beyond all imagining, of which love is the source. As Tagore, the Bengali author and poet of the last century, would have it: "Death is not extinguishing the light, but putting out the lamp because the dawn has come."

I believe the death-defying love of God, of which our capacity to give and receive love is an expression, draws those whose mortal life has ended into a new realm of love, in what Jesus calls "my Father's house," where there are "many dwelling places." A better translation is "stopping places," such as would be found along a caravan route. Indeed these stopping places were described by early commentators as stages in a person's ongoing journey beyond death into the ever-expanding realm of love, a journey of continual growth and discovery, of being and becoming, of being loved and loving.

As I increase in years, and I hope at the same time in wisdom and grace, the inevitability of death looms larger in my consciousness. When we are young, life is an open road yet to be traveled. Then, year follows year and various diminishments overtake us, reminding us of our mortality. As well, people who are bound to us through intimate ties of love and friendship cease to be as we have known them in this life. Such losses are difficult to bear as they drastically alter both our exterior and internal landscapes, and can leave us wounded and disoriented. Yet the very pain of grief is the sign of love, a love that endures. "Many waters cannot quench love," declares the Song of Solomon, "neither can floods drown it."

As the proper frame in which to place our lives is eternity, death is a point of transition, a doorway into a new mode of life and being. My aging, with its attendant losses in strength and energy, is part of a transition to a new state that lies on the other side of the grave.

"I am dying," a close friend of many years declared when I asked him the outcome of his latest appointment with his oncologist.

"I will travel with you as far as I can go," I replied.

And so began our journey. One day I asked him how he felt about knowing he was moving rather quickly toward the end of his time on earth. He had been a monk for almost all his adult life and I wondered what the fruit of his deep faith and years of intense prayer might provide to sustain him in the face of his impending death. After a long pause he replied, "I am scared because I don't know what lies on the other side of death. Even so, I am eager to find out."

During my friend's last days he was asked if he wanted to go to hospice. Without a moment's hesitation, he replied: "No, I want to go to heaven."

There are times when someone close to us who has died comes suddenly to mind. Perhaps they come to us in a dream, or speak to us in a voice we hear only in our minds. Perhaps just when it is most needed we hear a piece of music that is connected with them, or come across some object—a ring, a book, a photograph—that recalls a memory shot through with both sadness and love. At such times we may have a sense that the discovery was not random, but given as a sign of our enduring relationship with someone who has passed through the veil and is with us still. In such moments this life and the life beyond touch for an instant, and, in ways past anything we can understand or explain, we know that love never ends.

I think of people in congregations I have served who grieve the loss of a spouse saying, "I don't know what I will do now because he always took care of the finances," or "she was the one who always kept us in touch with our friends." I would often ask if they had thought of talking to their spouse and asking for help. This suggestion has frequently evoked shocked looks, so I remind them that the Book of Common Prayer speaks of our being "supported by this fellowship of love and prayer." I can't

say they had visions of the departed, but frequently when they
called upon that special person—"Donald, help me with . . . ."
or "Pam, what should I do about . . . "—they found themselves
enabled or illumined, or infused with unexpected confidence.
"It is as if Donald really heard me. I can't believe I am able to
do this!" To which I respond: "Well, I guess Donald is lending a
helping hand."

A Fellowship of Love and Prayer

> *For in the multitude of your saints you have surrounded*
> *us with a great cloud of witnesses, that we might rejoice in*
> *their fellowship . . .*
>   —Preface for the Feast of All Saints,
>   The Book of Common Prayer

Once during a class I was teaching for seminarians I caught
them by surprise when I asked them what the communion of
saints meant to them. It seemed a fair question given that they
affirmed their belief in it every time they said the Apostles'
Creed.

> *I believe in . . . the communion of saints . . .*

I was surprised by the blank looks all around the classroom.
I restated and repeated the question until finally one of the
students tentatively asked: "Does it mean that we are surrounded
by a great cloud of witnesses?"

Silence all around. Then I asked if they weren't aware that when
we say we believe in the communion of saints we are affirming
that Christ's life-giving love transcends death, and that we are
in communion with those who have gone before us: surrounded
and supported by them in a vast fellowship of love and prayer.
I pointed out that though we are pressed upon by this reality
that surrounds us, and invited to rejoice in their fellowship, the
communion of saints seems to many to be remote, distant, so
completely other that they hardly give it a thought.

This led the class into a broader discussion about our relationship to the communion of saints, that is, those who have died. After all, the term "saint" as it appears in the New Testament is a way of describing anyone who is faithful and is not restricted to those who have been formally declared saints. Indeed, many of those who appear in stained-glass windows and statuary were eccentric, flawed, and not easy to endure. St. Jerome was given to outbursts of anger and Francis of Assisi was a scandal to the people of his hometown. Sanctity is not necessarily about being perfect in some antiseptic way but about being available to God's purposes.

Over the years the communion of saints has allowed me to explore my ongoing relationship with deceased members of my own family who, as I remember them, were far from perfect and when they died left me with unresolved issues. My father's mother died during my years at the Church of the Redeemer in Bryn Mawr. To the end of her long life, Granny remained a formidable presence: demanding and critical and seldom one to utter a word of praise. One of my last visits with her before she died was in Newport, Rhode Island, where she spent the summers. She had broken her hip and was confined to a wheelchair so one of my duties was to accompany her to a nearby beach club and to push her chair along the boardwalk so she could enjoy the ocean air. One day as we made our way along we passed the cabaña of Mrs. Auchincloss, the mother-in-law of President Kennedy. Mrs. Auchincloss called out to my grandmother: "Oh Alice, dear, you must meet Jack." As the president put down the newspaper he was reading and came to greet us, Granny declared: "And this is my grandson. He went to Harvard and Oxford." Without missing a beat the president responded: "All he needs now is a state university."

This exchange was both amusing and a great embarrassment to me. Sometime after Granny's death, I was reminded of the occasion and how she had spoken of me with uncharacteristic enthusiasm. I then realized I had given her the opportunity to be proud and rejoice in her flesh and blood. I was able to see that, because of her disappointment in her son, and her alienation from her daughter, I had become the repository of the unrealized hopes and expectations she had long since abandoned for her own children. This insight allowed me to see her in a new and more compassionate light. I realized that her seeming severity, and what I perceived to be unwarranted criticism at times, was her effort to encourage me to make the best use of the gifts she saw within me. This new way of seeing her moved me to gratitude and I found myself saying aloud: "Thank you, Granny." My words then became a prayer that, delivered from the disappointments she carried in this life, she would be able now to discover what the psalmist meant by "the fullness of joy."

Several years later my father followed my grandmother into death. When he died from liver failure, the consequence of his alcoholism, I was both angry with him for what I perceived to be his self-inflicted demise, and relieved that I no longer was the "responsible adult" in the midst of his chaotic life. For many years after I thought of him only in terms of his failure to be a true father to me. I fixed him there, the prisoner of my anger and disappointment. And, then, I had a dream—and surely dreams can be instances of revelation and truth—in which my father came to me and said: "I did the best I could." When I woke up I somehow knew that, burdened by his problematic childhood, he most likely had done the best he could and, in spite of his burdens and brokenness, he had loved me. I realized, too, likely provoked by the dream, that just as I had changed and grown over the years since his death, so too had he. I had frozen him at a negative moment and overlooked the healing power of God's love and compassion, which I deeply believed had carried him forward into a new season of liberation allowing him to become more fully who, in the Divine Imagination, he was called to be. My dream allowed me to release him from the place of judgment where I had held him fast for so many years. In so doing, I, too, was set free.

Here I am put in mind of the words of Teilhard de Chardin: "For us God is eternal discovery and eternal growth." I often return to this affirmation that beyond death there is a process of continual becoming, of growth and discovery without end.

The Book of Revelation speaks of those who are faithful being given on the other side of death a white stone upon which is written a new name known only to God. This suggests to me that, in the words of St. Augustine, "we are a mystery even to our own selves." God alone knows us in the fullness of who God has called us to be. On the other side of death we continue to grow into that fullness of our personhood and to be given the white stone with our new, and true, name, which has been known only to God our creator. Then, born into eternity, we know ourselves as we have been fully known.

As I stand now between my birth and death and reflect upon all that has been thus far, I am filled with amazement and gratitude as I reread the scripture of my life, tracking down the Holy Ghost and trying to follow the lines of spiritual motion into that deep place where revelation takes place. Everywhere I see traces of the One I name and know as God who directly, and through countless others, has formed and guided me, challenged and sustained me, and led me along the way. I have sought to distill some of what I have found in the hope that it might encourage others to look for lines of spiritual motion in their own lives. I can think of no better way to end these reflections than to proclaim with St. Paul: *Glory to God whose power, working in us, can do infinitely more than we can ask or imagine.*

Sources and Citations

Author's Note: This is a partial list, arranged by chapter, of the sources from which quotations in the book were drawn. It is partial because over the years I have written down quotations that were meaningful to me, sometimes without noting where I had found them. The fact that many of them appeared just when I needed the insight they contained suggests to me that it was not so much that I found them, but that they, and their author, found me. Believing that nothing is accidental, I look upon such moments of discovery as the work of the Spirit. My life has been deeply enriched by friends in the Spirit, both living and dead, whose wisdom and witness have been manna along the way. It is my hope that the quotations and references in these pages will introduce you to new friends in the Spirit as well.

To the Reader

"You have made us for yourself, O Lord, and our heart is restless until it rests in you." From *Confessions*, written by St. Augustine of Hippo (354–430), a theologian and philosopher who was a bishop in North Africa and whose *Confessions* and other writings continue to nourish and inform present-day pilgrims and seekers.

Listening to Your Life

"We seek you, O God, because you have already found us." St. Augustine, *Tractates, Homilies and Sermons on John*: Tractate 7:21

"How can you draw close to God if you are far from your own self?" St. Augustine, *Confessions*

"A simple openness to the next human moment brings us into union with God in Christ." This quote is from *Merton's Palace of Nowhere*, a book by James Finley, a disciple of Thomas Merton.

"Too few people have experienced the divine image as the innermost possession of their souls. Christ only meets them from without—never from within the soul." Carl Jung quoted by Frieda Fordham, *An Introduction to Jung's Psychology*

"By means of all created things, without exception, the Divine assails us, penetrates us and molds us." This quote of the French Jesuit priest, paleontologist, and philosopher Pierre Teilhard de Chardin is from his book, *The Divine Milieu.*

The observation by Evelyn Underhill, an English mystic of the last century, that there is no such thing as coincidence, but rather God's universe caught in the act of rhyming, has been a touchstone for me. Her books on mysticism and worship continue to be published along with many of her books on the spiritual life and prayer. For her, mysticism was far from esoteric and was very much rooted in daily life. "Homely," in the English sense of plain, practical, or down to earth, was one of Underhill's favorite ways of describing God's way with us.

Gathering the Fragments

"For the glory of God is a human person fully alive, and the life of humanity consists in the vision of God." This quote is from Irenaeus (130–202), who was the Bishop of Lyon. It is from *Against the Heresies* and is cited in *Celebrating the Saints* by Robert Atwell.

Eric Hoffer's observation about change being experienced at the visceral level is included in his book *The Ordeal of Change.*

In 1984, shortly after I was elected Bishop Coadjutor of Chicago, I came across an article by Alan Jones entitled, "The Bishop as Martyr." As I remember it, the article explored the cost of being a bishop in terms of relinquishment of self in service to others.

It described episcopal ministry as a form of being stretched and obliged to widen one's embrace, and in the process having to face one's limitations. The article included a quotation by Roman Catholic Brazilian Archbishop Dom Hélder Câmara. His challenging words became an invitation to me.

Encountering the Divine

The notion that the world is news of God is from a meditation by Gerard Manley Hopkins included in *Notes on the Principle and Foundation* (1882). The full meditation is as follows:

> God's utterance of God within God is God the Word,
> God's utterance outside of God is this world.
> This world then is word, expression, news of God.
> Therefore its end, purpose, purport, meaning is God,
> and its life or work to name and praise God . . .
> The world and humanity, each after its own manner
> should give God being in return
> for the being God has given it.

Hopkins's poem, *God's Grandeur*, begins with this line: *"The world is charged with the grandeur of God."*

Joseph Addison said that his hymn, "The Spacious Firmament on High," composed in 1712, was inspired by Psalm 19. Psalm 19:1 is sometimes rendered as: "The heavens declare the glory of God; the skies proclaim the work of his hands."

The advice to "pray simply" is from a Russian Orthodox monk, Macarius of Optina (1788–1860). I came across it in a book about Russian Orthodox saints and holy days. I photocopied the page, but forgot to write down the title of the book. Given our western preoccupation with achievement, his words are a counterbalance and a release from a tendency to evaluate prayer in the very act of praying. They remind me of Paul's declaration (Romans 8) that we don't know how to pray, but that the Spirit prays within us and helps us in our weakness.

These words of Father Benson are quoted in *Benson of Cowley* by Martin Smith: "Our role in prayer is not to try to raise ourselves to God by the violence of natural effort, but to surrender, to cooperate in the movement by which the Holy Spirit rises to the Father."

The conversation between St. Seraphim of Sarov and Nicholas Motovilov, as written by Motovilov, is included in *A Treasury of Russian Spirituality*, edited by G.P. Fedotow (1886–1951).

Acquiring a Heart: The Complexity of Being Fully Human

The reflection on a merciful heart by St. Isaac of Syria is from "Homily 81," included in various collections of his writings.

Knowing as We Are Known

"For us God is eternal discovery and eternal growth." Pierre Teilhard de Chardin, *The Divine Milieu*